WHITALL, TATUM & CO.

WHITALL, TATUM & CO.
1880

Flint Glassware, Blue Ware, Perfume and Cologne Bottles, Show Bottles and Globes, Green Glassware, Stoppers, Druggists' Sundries

Illustrated Catalog and Historical Introduction

AMERICAN HISTORICAL CATALOG COLLECTION

THE PYNE PRESS
Princeton

All Rights Reserved

Copyright © 1971 by The Pyne Press

No part of this publication may be reproduced
or transmitted in any form or by any means,
electronic or mechanical, including
photocopy, recording, or any information storage
and retrieval system, without permission
in writing from the publisher.

First edition

Library of Congress Catalog Card Number 74–146206

ISBN 0–87861–004–9

Printed in the United States of America

Note to the Reader. Reproduction of copy and line drawings are as faithful to the original as is technically possible. Broken type and lines which are uneven or broken can be spotted; these are original! You will understand that manufacturers of such products as woodenware, tinware, glassware and weathervanes were not dedicated to the fine art of printing or involved in the business of publishing. All American Historical Catalog Collection editions are photographed in facsimile from the best available copy, are printed on an especially receptive offset paper, and are strongly bound.

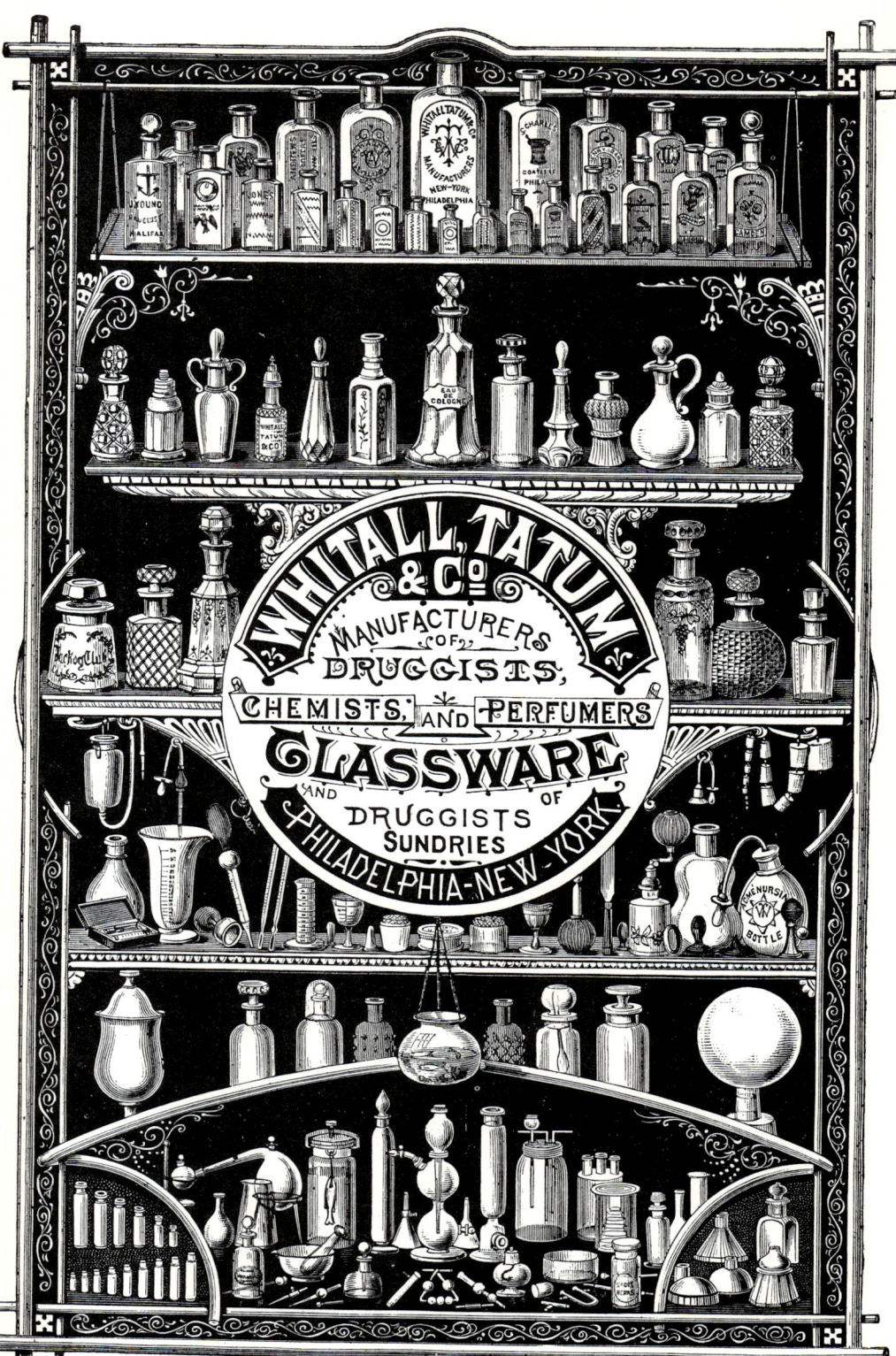

WHITALL, TATUM & CO.

GLASS MANUFACTURERS.

Druggists', Chemists' and Perfumers'

GLASSWARE.

DRUGGISTS' SUNDRIES.

No. 410 Race Street,	46 AND 48 Barclay Street,
P. O. Box 2712,	P. O. Box 3814,
PHILADELPHIA.	NEW YORK.

CONTENTS.

	PAGE.
STOPPERS	6
STYLES OF FINISH	7
PRIVATE MOULDS AND LETTERED PLATES	7–11
FLINT GLASSWARE	12–18
BLUE WARE	19
PERFUMERY AND COLOGNES	20–24
POMADES AND GLASS BOXES	25
SHOP FURNITURE AND PRESCRIPTION-DESK FURNITURE	26–29
HOMEOPATHIC VIALS	30, 31
SHOW BOTTLES AND GLOBES	32
CHEMICAL WARE	33–44
GREEN GLASSWARE	45–50
FRUIT JARS	50
DRUGGISTS' SUNDRIES	51–69
CUT AND ENGRAVED COLOGNES	70–71
SCALES	72

INDEX.

	PAGE.
Acids	28, 48
Acid Drop Bottles	40
Adapters	38
Anatomical Jars	44
Aquaria	32
Aspirator Bottles	18
Assay Flasks	36
Atomizers—Cologne, Throat, Nasal	60
Ball Neck Panels	16, 46
Balsams	27
Barbers' 18 oz. Bottle	71
Battery Jars	43
Beaker Glasses	36
Bed Pans	67
Bell Glasses	43
Bird Bottles, Baths, &c.	18
Blakes	13, 47
Blue Ware	19, 27
Bougies	61
Boxes, Opal and Glass	25, 43, 60
Boxes, Paper and Wood Lined	61
Brackets	62
Brandy Fruits	49
Breast Shields and Breast Pumps	55
Bulbs, Rubber	55
Bung Thieves	18
Calomels	18, 48
Carboys	50
Carmine Inks	16, 48
Case Vials	31
Castor Oils	18, 19, 46, 47
Catheters	61
Catsup Flasks	49
Caustics	48
Chemical Ware	33–44
Chlorals	18
Chloride of Calcium Tubes and Jars	39, 42
Chlorodyne	19
Chloroforms	18, 27

	PAGE
Citrates	18, 19, 48
Club Sauce	49
Cod Liver Oils	18, 46
Coin Test Bottles	40
Cold Cream	25, 63
Colognes	24, 70, 71
Comparison Tubes	37
Confectionery Jars	32
Contents of Packages	4, 12
Corks	68, 69
Cork Presses and Cork Screws	68, 69
Counter Urns	32
Crystal Nursing Bottle Fittings	54
Cupping Glasses	55
Demijohns	50
Dentists' Spittoon Funnels	18
Dental Syringes	59
Desiccating Jars	43
Dishes, Chemical	39
Douches, Nasal	56
Drawer Pulls	62
Dropping Glasses	39
Druggists' Sundries	52–69
Ear Cleaners and Ear Syringes	55, 59
English Essential Oils	18, 19, 48
Engraved Colognes	70, 71
Ethers	27
Evaporating Dishes	42, 66
Eye Baths and Eye Syringes	59
Fever Thermometers	61
Filter Racks	69
Finger Cots	55
Finish, Styles of	7
Fish Globes	32
Flasks, Chemical and Measuring	36, 64
Flavoring Extracts	16, 20–22
Florida Water	48
Fluted Prescriptions	16, 45
Fountain Nasal Douches and Syringes	56, 59

INDEX.

	PAGES.
FRENCH SQUARES	13, 19, 47
FRUIT JARS	49–50
FUNNELS	38, 67
GALLIPOTS	25, 63
GAS BOTTLES	38
GAS GENERATORS	40
GLYCERINE	18, 48
GRADUATES, PHENIX AND VON HOFE	64–65
GRUEL TUBES	56
HOMEOPATHIC FRENCH SQUARES AND VIALS	13, 30, 31
HONEY	18, 50
HORSE RADISH	45, 49
HYACINTH GLASSES	18
HYPODERMIC SYRINGES	61
HYDROMETER JARS	44
IGNITION TUBES	37, 38
INKS, INK WELLS AND INDELIBLES	16, 48
INSECT BOTTLES	44
INSECT POWDER BOTTLES AND GUNS	48, 54
JARS, MUSEUM	44
JELLIES	49
JUG HANDLE BOTTLES	20–23
LABELS, GLASS	27, 71
LEECH TUBES AND JARS	55, 66
LEMON SYRUPS	46
LETTERED PLATES	8–11
LIPS, BOTTLE	7
LITER FLASKS	36, 64
LUBINS	20, 22
MEDICINE TUBES AND DROPPERS	56, 69
do GLASSES	64
METRIC PRESCRIPTIONS	15
MILK JARS	18
MILLVILLE ROUND	12
do CHEMICAL JARS	40
do FRUIT JARS	50
MINERALS	49
MOLASSES SAMPLES	18
MORPHINES	18
MORTARS AND PESTLES	40, 67
MOULDS AND PLATES	7–11
MUCILAGE	16, 48
MUSEUM JARS	44
MUSTARDS	18, 49
NASAL ATOMIZERS	60
do DOUCHES, POWDER DOUCHE AND SYRINGES	56
NIPPLES, NIPPLE SHELLS AND SHIELDS	54, 55
NURSING BOTTLES	17, 48, 52, 53
do FITTINGS	54, 55
OCTAGONS	18, 47
OIL SAMPLES	18
OINTMENT POTS AND JARS	25, 63, 66
OPAL BOXES	25, 63, 66
OVALS	13, 46
OXYGEN GLOBES	37
PAINT JARS	18, 48
PACKING BOTTLES	19, 47
PANELS	16, 46
PATCH BOXES	25, 63, 66
PATENT MEDICINES	47
PEPPER SAUCE	49
PERCOLATERS AND WEIGHTS	42, 64
PERFUMERS' WARE	20–25, 70, 71
PHILADELPHIA OVALS	12, 15, 46
PICKLE JARS	49
PILL MACHINES AND PILL TILES	67, 69
PIPETTES, CHEMICAL	39
PIPETTES, FRENCH AND EXACT	56
PLATES, FOR LETTERING	8–11
do GROUND GLASS	39
POISONS	19
POMADES	25, 63
PORTERS	49
POTASH BULBS	39
POWDERS	14
PRECIPITATING JARS	42
PRESCRIPTION BOTTLES	12–15, 19, 45, 46
PRESCRIPTION CASE BOTTLES	28, 29
do PIPETTES	64
PRESERVING JARS	49, 50
PROBANGS	55
PROOF GLASSES	40
QUININES	18
REAGENT BOTTLES	34, 35
RECEIVERS AND RETORTS	37
RODS, GLASS	40
SACHET BOTTLES	71
SADDLE-BAG VIALS	16
SALT MOUTHS	14, 26–29, 35
SAMPLE BOTTLES	18
SCALES	72
SCHNAPPS	50
SELTZERS OR PACKERS	19, 47
SEWING MACHINE OIL	18
SHAPES, DESIGNATION OF	7
SHOP FURNITURE AND PRES. CASE FURNITURE	26–29, 32
SHOW BOTTLES	32, 42, 43
SNUFFS	49
SPATULAS	67
SPECIE JARS	32
SPECIMEN BOTTLES	43
SPIRIT LAMPS	40
SPITTOON FUNNELS	18
SPOON TOPS TO BOTTLES	28
SPRINKLERS AND SPRINKLE-TOP BOTTLES	21, 22, 23, 24, 62, 63, 71
STIRRING RODS	56
STOP COCKS	38
STOPPERS	6
STOPPERED BOTTLES	6, 13, 14, 16, 20–29, 48, 70, 71
SUNDRIES, DRUGGISTS'	51–69
SWEET OILS	49
SYPHONS	38
SYRINGES	57–59
SYRUPS	27
TEETHING PADS, RINGS, &c.	55
TEST TUBES	37, 38
THERMOMETERS, FEVER	61
THROAT ATOMIZERS	60
TINCTURES	14, 26–29, 34, 35
TOOTH POWDERS	16, 22, 23, 25, 63
TOOTHACHE DROPPERS	61
TUBING U. T. & Y. AND CHEMICAL	39–41
do RUBBER	55
TUBULATURE, BOTTLES WITH	42
UNION OVALS	13, 46
URINALS	67
URINOMETERS	59
VARNISH	48
WATCH GLASSES	42
WEIGHING BOTTLES	39
WEIGHT OF BOTTLES	7
WINE BOTTLES	50
WOULFF BOTTLES	40
YEAST POWDERS	48

TABLE

SHOWING THE NUMBER OF *DOZENS* USUALLY PACKED IN EACH BOX OF FLINT AND GREEN WARE.

	½ oz	1 oz	2 oz	3 oz	4 oz	6 oz	8 oz	10 oz	12 oz	16 oz	24 oz	qt	3 pt	½ gl
Prescriptions. Round Shouldered, Boston, Fluted long, and Wide Mouth	72	72	60	48	48	30	24	...	18	12	...	8	...	...
Ovals and Union Ovals, French Square Prescriptions, Philadelphia Ovals	72	72	60	48	36	30	24	...	18	12	10	8	...	...
Stoppered, Round and French Square	72	60	60	48	36	30	24	...	12	12	8	6	...	...
Panels	72	72	60	48	36	24	18	18	15	12	10	...	...	...
Ball Neck Panel	72	60	60	36	36	24	18	...	...	...	...	...	...	...
Blakes	72	72	60	48	36	30	24	...	18	12	...	...	...	...
Round Extracts, Lubins, &c	72	60	...	...	...	...	...	...	...	...	...	...	...	...
Castor Oils	...	...	60	48	36	24	18	18	18	12	10	...	...	...
Oval Castor Oils	...	...	60	...	36	...	18	...	12	...	...	...	...	...
Cod Liver Oils	...	...	...	...	36	...	18	...	15	12	...	...	...	...
Seltzers, Wide and Narrow Mouth	...	...	...	...	...	...	24	...	12	10	8	4	4	
Extra Seltzers, Wide and Narrow Mouth	...	...	...	...	...	18	...	12	12	10	8	4	4	
Acids	...	...	...	...	...	...	18	...	12	12	...	8	...	4
Pyramid Inks	...	72	60	...	...	...	...	...	...	...	...	...	...	...
Round Inks	...	...	60	...	48	30	24	...	12	...	8	...	...	...
Indelible and Mordant Inks, Gen. Essence, Harlem Oils, British Oils, S. Flat Bear's Oils	72 doz.													
L. Bear's Oils, Turlingtons, Godfrey's, Opos	60 doz.													
Varnish	48 doz.													
9 oz. Citrate	18 doz.													
12 oz. Citrate	12 doz.													

Contents of Assorted Cases.

	One Gross Cases.	Five Gross Cases.
½ oz.	3 Doz.	9 Doz.
1 oz.	4 Doz.	18 Doz.
2 oz.	3 Doz.	16 Doz.
4 oz.	1 Doz.	7 Doz.
6 oz.	½ Doz.	4 Doz.
8 oz.	½ Doz.	6 Doz.

No Charge for Original Packages.

WHITALL, TATUM & CO.
PHILADELPHIA AND NEW YORK.

We necessarily send our Catalogue to many parties with whom we have not the pleasure of an acquaintance; and persons ordering goods for the first time from us will please accompany their orders with the cash or satisfactory references.

No goods sent per express, C. O. D., to strangers, on account of the additional expense to us in case of non-acceptance by the purchaser.

Estimates made, and special quotations furnished, when desired.

All ware on the list can be furnished stoppered on special orders. Also in Flint, Green, Dark Green, Blue, Amber, or Opaque.

In ordering Glassware, customers will kindly state whether they wish Flint or Green; and when the ware is to be stoppered, specify particularly the style of stopper wanted. (See page 6.)

TERMS:—*Payment in funds at par in New York or Philadelphia.*

ORDERS FOR SUMMER STOCK.

But little Glass can be made in Summer, owing to the heat. It is therefore desirable that our customers, in order to procure a stock of Glassware to meet their wants *during the Summer*, should *so far as practicable*, send in their orders by the 1st of 5th month (May) in each year.

FLINT GLASS WARE.

NO CHARGE FOR ORIGINAL PACKAGES.

A LIBERAL DISCOUNT TO THE TRADE.

1880.

We desire to call the attention of the Trade to our Flint Glass, which has been used for many years by most of the leading Wholesale and Retail Druggists in New York, Philadelphia, Boston, Baltimore, Chicago, St. Louis, Louisville, New Orleans, and San Francisco, as well as by English Perfumers, to their entire satisfaction, and we recommend it with confidence as a reliable and excellent substitute for the much more expensive glass made with lead.

We believe it superior to glass of the same kind made in any country, and invite those who have not used it to give it a trial, and compare the color, style of finish, and amount of breakage with that received from other sources. As we regularly keep on hand the largest stock on this Continent, we are able to fill orders promptly from our houses in either New York or Philadelphia.

Assorted boxes, containing six sizes, from half-ounce to eight ounce inclusive, and holding one or five gross of either Round-Shouldered Prescriptions, Union Ovals, French Squares, or Philadelphia Ovals, will be sold at the usual discount as samples. For assortment, see page 4.

For GREEN GLASS see page 45.

Boxes containing a line of labeled samples will be sent at a nominal price, upon application.

STOPPERED WARE.

We are making a specialty of STOPPERED WARE, which we have great confidence in recommending as very reliable for Essences and volatile fluids, or for packing with liquid contents, as every bottle is carefully tested before it is sent out. For card prices, see pages 14, 20, &c.

STOPPERED PRESCRIPTION BOTTLES.

Some of the leading Druggists are now furnishing STOPPERED BOTTLES to their customers for Prescriptions. Where a bottle stands for days or weeks on a patient's table, the stopper is a great convenience, as well as ornament. For styles of stoppers, see below.

It is desirable to tie the stopper down, or to send the bottle closed with a cork, leaving the glass-stopper tied to the neck till it reaches the patient, as stoppers can be loosened by rough carrying. The net *extra* cost of stoppers on the smaller sizes is under three cents per bottle. See Catalogue, with discount.

Persons having engraved plates with us can have three dozen or upwards of any size stoppered, when we are making their lettered ware of *the same size*.

STOPPERS.

Ext. Lubin Style Ball Stopper.

We have Stoppers appropriated to Tinctures and Saltmouths, as well as to the different styles of Perfumery and other ware, but we can insert other descriptions of stoppers to meet special orders. When ware is to have any other than the usual stopper, it should be described by number,— 702, &c.

701. Mushroom Tincture. All sizes.
    702. Ball. All sizes.
703. Flat Head. All sizes.
    704. Square Head. ½ oz. to Quarts.
705. Lubin. ½, 1 and 2 oz.
    { 706. Tall.
    { 707. Hollow Tall. All sizes.
708. Pointed. 1 ounce.
    709. Mushroom Salt Mouth. All sizes.
711. Syrup Loose. ½ Pints to Gallons.
    712. Carmine. All sizes.
713. Teat Carmine. ½ oz. to Pint.
    714. Hood. All sizes.
715. Fancy Hollow. ¼ Pints to Quarts.
    716. Cone. ½ and 1 oz.

717. Pear.   All sizes.
718. Medicine Chest. ¾ and 2 oz.
719. Chloral. ½ and 1 ounce.
720. Table. ½ to 2 oz.
721. Brilliant. 1 and 2 oz.
722. Club Sauce. ½ Pint and Pint.
723. Screw Ball Stopper. ½ and 1 oz.
724. Flat Hood Stopper. All sizes.
725. Oblong Head Stop'r. 1 oz. to Quart.
726. Acorn Stopper. 1 to 8 oz.
727. Globe Hollow. All sizes.
729. See Cut 556. Perfumery List. 4 and 8 oz.
730. Dome Serrated. 8 and 16 oz.
731. Umbrella. 8 and 16 oz.
728. } 8 oz. {
732. } 2 oz. { Tall
733. } 4 oz. { Hexagon.
734. } ½ Pint. { Hollow.
735. } Pint. { Flat Cut.
736.—741. S. & L. Lapidary— see Cut 563. All sizes.

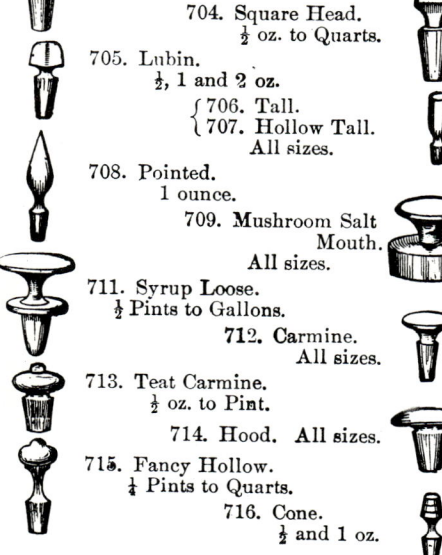
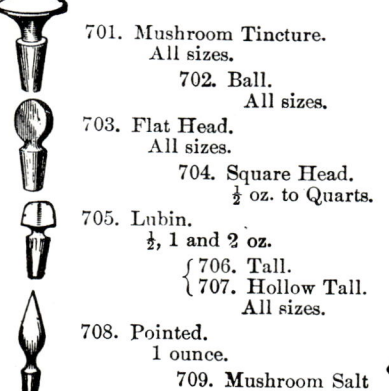

STYLES OF FINISH.

When ware is desired with a different finish from the standard style it should be distinctly indicated as below.

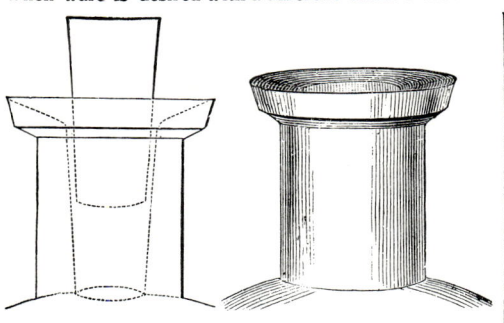

"**Blow Over**" means ground off without lip.

"**Deep Lip**" means a flat patent lip, as put on English Essential Oils.

"**Trumpet Mouth**" is used in Colognes.

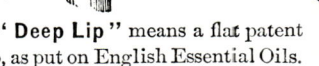

"**Prescription Lip**" means a flaring mouth, with thin edge, suitable for dropping.

"**Champagne Finish**" means that a narrow ring is below the mouth.

"**Extract Lip**"—"**Colgate Style**" —this style is used in bulk and small extract.

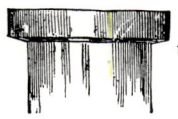

"**P. L.**" means "Patent Lip," that is, square, and flat on top.

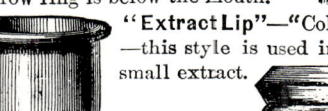

"**Double Ring**" means a ring such as in Ayer's Ware.

"**Wide Prescription Lip**" means extra width of thin lip, as in Re-agent bottles.

"**Ring**" means a finish such as is generally used on Castor Oils.

SHAPES.

T. means Tall Style.		**B. N.** means Ball Neck.		**N. S.** means New Style.	
L. " Large Size.		**P. O.** " Pour Out.		**O. S.** " Old Style.	
M. " Medium Size.		**P.** " Plain on one side, with only 3 panels.		**W. M.** " Wide Mouth.	
S. " Small Size.				**S. F.** " Shop Furniture.	
L. L. " Long and Large.		**C.** " Cylinder Style mould, larger at shoulder than at base.		**I. M.** " Iron Mould.	
H. " High.					

WEIGHT OF GLASS.

Our Ware is made at good ordinary weight, which is, on the whole, the safest, and shows the contents to best advantage. By the general use of scales in our factories, great uniformity of weight, and consequently of content, is secured. When desired we can make Ware of extra weight. As a rule 3 ozs. of solid glass by weight displaces about 1 oz. of water.

NEW MOULDS.

Large additions will be found in this Catalogue to our lists of Shop Furniture, Sundries, Perfumery, Colognes, Pomades, &c. We are constantly adding new styles in the various departments, and call special attention to the extension of our line of moulds for the insertion of lettered plates. (See pages 8 and 9.)

DIRECTIONS FOR ORDERING PRIVATE MOULDS.

As we have two large shops for making Bottle Moulds, we are prepared to execute orders on favorable terms. The advantages are great for making moulds at a Glass Factory where experts know the special requirements of a mould that will deliver smooth and regular bottles. When desired, samples can be blown and forwarded before lettering or finishing up the mould, so as to allow of modification of style.

In ordering moulds, it is well to select a bottle as near as possible to the kind desired, and to send it with directions for any variations to be made in the new mould. In addition to shape, note also content, finish, whether common or extra weight, and whether lettered or unlettered.

As graduates vary greatly, we would ask, where possible, to receive a bottle containing the exact quantity required in the new bottle, MEASURED UP TO THE BOTTOM OF THE NECK. For any unusual shape, a wooden model is desirable.

Prices of new moulds vary with the amount of work expended on them. Estimates will be promptly forwarded on application.

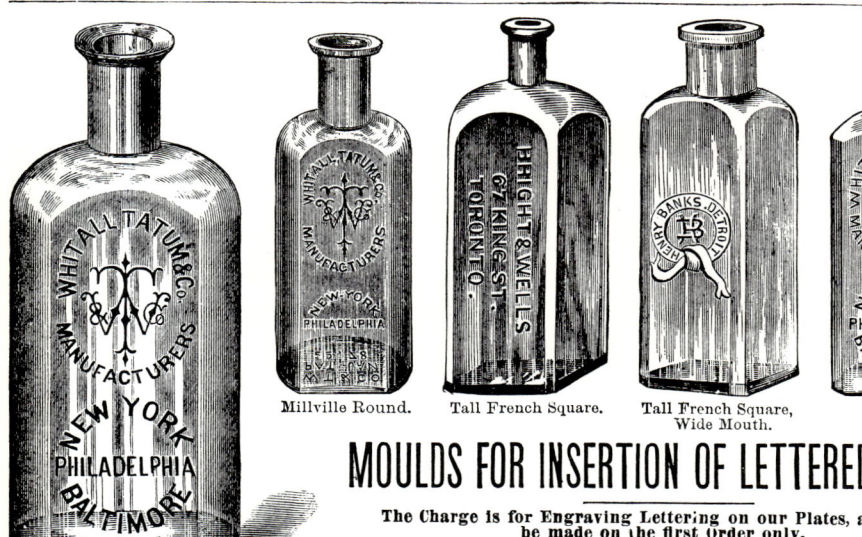

Millville Round.   Tall French Square.   Tall French Square, Wide Mouth.   Blake.

New Philadelphia Oval.

MOULDS FOR INSERTION OF LETTERED PLATES.

The Charge is for Engraving Lettering on our Plates, and it will be made on the first Order only.

We have the following sets of moulds prepared for the insertion of names without the expense of making a new mould for each new name to be inserted Special pencil designs, with devices, monograms, &c., will be sent for selection or approval without charge.

We can make a rectangular, oval or gothic **Panel**, on the lettered side of the **French Square**, or on the flat side of the **Philadelphia Oval** and **Millville Round**. (See page 13.) The effect of the Panel is to reduce the content to very nearly the name. Thus, we make the 4 ounce French Square Prescription to hold say 4¼ ounces to the bottom of the neck, but with one side a panel it would hold only 4 ounces.

PHILADELPHIA OVALS.
    MILLVILLE ROUND.
        FRENCH SQUARES.
            FRENCH SQUARES, WIDE MOUTH.
                BLAKES AND TALL ENGLISH BLAKES.

*** The same Plates fit into each of the first four above Styles of Moulds, and Ware from the same engraved plate can be ordered of either of these shapes of bottles.

PRICE ONE DOLLAR AND FIFTY CENTS TO SIX DOLLARS EACH FOR ENGRAVING,

Moulds fitted for Plates are prepared for the following shapes and sizes:

PHILADELPHIA OVAL.	MILLVILLE ROUND.	TALL FRENCH SQUARE.	WIDE MOUTH FRENCH SQUARE.	BLAKE.	TALL BLAKE.
		1 drachm.		1½ drachm.	
		2 drachm.			
		3 drachm.		¼ ounce.	
½ ounce.	½ ounce.	½ & B. ½ oz.	½ ounce.	½ ounce.	
1 ounce.	1 ounce.	1 oz. & B. 1 oz.	1 ounce.	1 ounce.	1 ounce.
		High 1 ounce.			
		1¼ ounce.			
1½ ounce.		1½ ounce.	1½ ounce.		
		High 2 ounce.			
2 ounce.	2 ounce.	2 oz. & B. 2 oz.	2 ounce.	2 ounce.	2 ounce.
3 ounce.	3 ounce.	3 ounce.	3 ounce.	3 ounce.	3 ounce.
4 oz.; also 2 flat plates.	4 ounce.	4 oz. & B. 4 oz.	4 ounce.	4 ounce.	4 ounce.
		5 ounce.	6 ounce.		
5 ounce.	6 ounce.	6 ounce.	7½ ounce.	6 ounce.	6 ounce.
6 ounce.	8 ounce.	8 ounce.	8 ounce.	8 ounce.	8 ounce.
8 ounce.		10 ounce.	10 ounce.	10 ounce.	10 ounce.
10 ounce.	12 ounce.	12 ounce.	12 ounce.	12 ounce.	
12 ounce.		14 ounce.	15 ounce.		
16 ounce.	16 ounce.	16 ounce.	16 ounce.	16 ounce.	16 ounce
		24 ounce.	20 ounce.		
		28 ounce.			
32 ounce.		32 ounce.			

For Lettered Plates of the Metric Measure Philadelphia Ovals, see Page 15.

MOULDS for INSERTION of LETTERED PLATES.

Round Shoulder Prescription.

Union Oval.

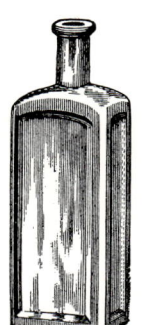
Panel.

Cod Liver.

Ball Neck Panel.

ROUND SHOULDER PRESCRIPTION.	RE-AGENT STYLE. See page 34.	ROUND WIDE MOUTH.	UNION OVALS.
½ oz.	Narrow Mouth.		½ oz.
1 oz.	1 oz.	1 oz.	1 oz.
2 oz.	4 oz.		2 oz.
3 oz.	6 oz.		3 oz.
4 oz.	8 oz.	4 oz.	4 oz.
6 oz.	16 oz.	7 oz. (Calomel.)	6 oz.
8 oz.	**BOTTOM LETTERING.**		8 oz.
12 oz.	Names can be put at small cost on the bottoms of any mould without the expense of making the rest of mould.	14 oz. (Calomel.)	12 oz.
16 oz.		**TOOTH POWDER.**	16 oz.
B. 16 oz. (Tall with High Shoulders.)		902. 1½ oz. Oblong.	32 oz.
B. 32 oz. (Tall with High Shoulders.)		903. 3 oz. Oblong.	**O. S. SHORT FR. SQ.**
			16 oz.
PANELS.	**BALL NECK PANELS.**	**COD LIVER PANELS.**	**SQUARES, EXTRA WIDE MOUTH.**
5 drachm.	½ oz.	Balt. 1½ oz.	
Tall 6 drachm.	7 drachm.	2 oz.	7½ oz.
Small 1 oz.	1 oz.	B. 3 oz.	15 oz.
Large 1 oz.	1¼ oz.	4 oz.	**CITRATE MAGNESIA.**
1¼ oz.	1½ oz.	B. 4 oz.	
Small 1¼ oz.	1¾ oz.	7 oz.	12 oz.
1½ oz.	Tall 2 oz.	8 oz.	**GRANULATED CITRATE.**
L. 2 oz. & Balt. P. 2 oz.	3 oz.	B. 8 oz.	
T., & P. 2 oz. (3 Panels.	Small 4 oz.	16 oz.	5 oz.
Small 3 oz.	Broad 4 oz.		**OCTAGON.**
T., & P. 3 oz. (3 Panels.)	5 oz.	**PERFUMERY.**	
High 3 oz.	6 oz.	816. 2 oz. Fancy B. N. Panel.	3 oz.
High 4 oz.	8 oz.	836. 1 oz. Oval Panel Cologne.	**CALOMEL.**
Tall 4 oz. (3 Panels.)	**NURSING BOTTLES.**		7 oz.
Plain 4 oz. (3 Panels.)	Bent Neck and Round Bottom.	862. ½ oz. Lubin Panel.	14 oz.
5 oz.		861. 1 oz. Lubin Panel.	
Small 6 oz.		863. 2 oz. Lubin Panel.	**ESSENTIAL OILS.**
Tall 6 oz. (3 Panels.)		886. Tall 1 oz. Panel Col.	(Lettered Shoulders to Moulds.)
P. & T. 8 oz. (3 Panels.)	**FLAVORING EXTRACTS.**	889. 1 oz. Cone, 3 Panels.	½ Pint.
High 8 oz.		897. 2 oz. Caswell Panel.	Pint.
High 12 oz.	2 oz. Ext. (Burnett style.)		Quart.
Broad 12 oz. (3 Panels.)	4 oz. Ext. (Burnett style.)		
14 oz.			

     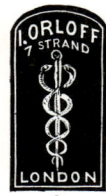  

     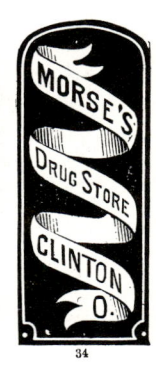

DESIGNS FOR LETTERED PLATES.

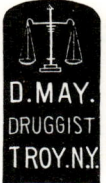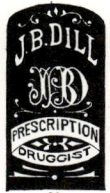
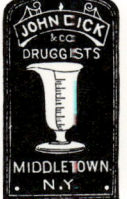
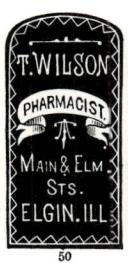
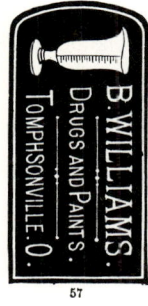
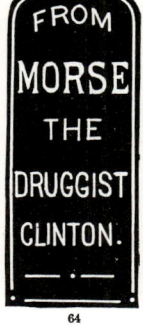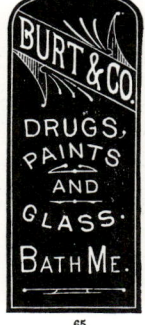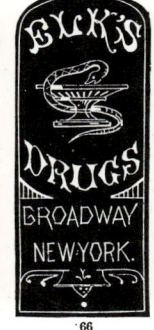

FLINT PRESCRIPTION BOTTLES.

SUBJECT TO DISCOUNT.

The content of the ½ and 1 ounce Prescription Bottles is as near as can be ½ and 1 ounce. On the larger sizes we approximate in content as nearly as possible to five per cent. above the name, measuring always to the base of neck of the bottle. Thus 4 ounce contains about 4¼ ounces, and 8 ounce 8⅓ ounces.

The quantity of Flint Prescription Bottles in an Original Package is as follows: a package of lettered ware may vary a trifle from this table, however, as it is impossible, when blowing, to foresee the number of bottles that will be fit to pack.

½ ounce . . . . 6 gross.	6 ounce . . . . 2½ gross.
1 ounce . . . . 6 gross.	8 ounce . . . . 2 gross.
2 ounce . . . . 5 gross.	12 ounce . . . . 1½ gross.
3 ounce . . . . 4 gross.	16 ounce . . . . 1 gross.
4 ounce Fr. Sq. and Ph. Oval . . 3 gross.	32 ounce . . . . ⅔ gross.
4 ounce R. S. . . . . 3 gross.	

NO CHARGE FOR ORIGINAL PACKAGES.

For Discounts from List inquire by Mail.

THE SAME LETTERED PLATES fit into the moulds for **PHILADELPHIA OVALS, FRENCH SQUARES, FRENCH SQUARES WIDE MOUTH,** and **MILLVILLE ROUND PRESCRIPTIONS.**

For **STOPPERED PRESCRIPTIONS,** see Page 6.   For **CORKS,** see Page 66.   For **LETTERED PLATES,** see Page 8.

Millville Round Prescriptions.

PATENTED JANUARY 22, 1878.

Taking the *same plates* used for FRENCH SQUARE PRESCRIPTIONS and PHILADELPHIA OVALS.

This style has the recommendation of entire novelty, a flat lettered side adapted to packing, and of a base not easily overturned.

	℔ gross.
½ ounce	$3 00
1 ounce	3 75
2 ounce	4 75
3 ounce	5 50
4 ounce	7 00
6 ounce	8 50
8 ounce	10 50
12 ounce	13 75
16 ounce	16 50

Philadelphia Ovals.

Flat on One Side,

This style combines the following advantages. It has no sharp corners, which are apt to break and collect deposits. It can be carried conveniently in the pocket, and will take a large label, which can be read without turning the bottle.

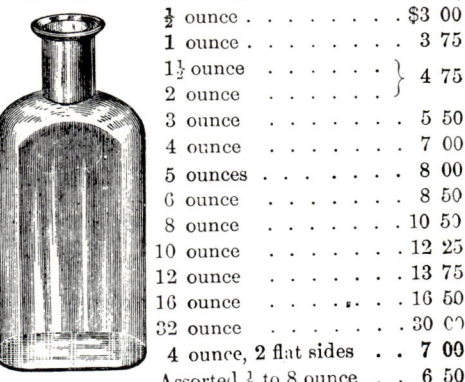

	℔ gross
½ ounce	$3 00
1 ounce	3 75
1½ ounce . . . . . . }	4 75
2 ounce . . . . }	
3 ounce	5 50
4 ounce	7 00
5 ounces	8 00
6 ounce	8 50
8 ounce	10 50
10 ounce	12 25
12 ounce	13 75
16 ounce	16 50
32 ounce	30 00
4 ounce, 2 flat sides . .	7 00
Assorted ½ to 8 ounce . .	6 50

TALL FRENCH SQUARE PRESCRIPTIONS.

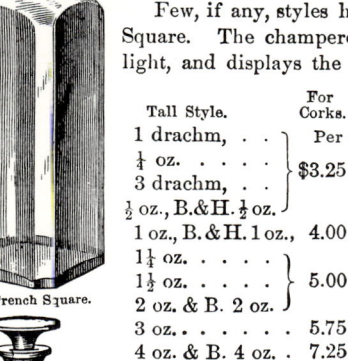
Tall French Square.

The Lettered Plates for the French Square Prescriptions fit also the French Square Wide Mouth moulds, the "Millville Round," and the Philadelphia Oval. See page 10.

Few, if any, styles have held the favor of the public so long as the Tall French Square. The champered edges make an octagon with angles, which reflects the light, and displays the contents to great advantage.

Tall Style.	For Corks.	Stoppered.
	Per Gross.	
1 drachm,		
¼ oz.	} $3.25	$10.00
3 drachm,		
½ oz., B.&H. ½ oz.		
1 oz., B.&H. 1 oz.,	4.00	11.00
1¼ oz.	} 5.00	12.50
1½ oz.		
2 oz. & B. 2 oz.		
3 oz.	5.75	15.00
4 oz. & B. 4 oz.	7.25	17.00
5 oz.	8.25	18.50
6 oz.	9.00	20.00
8 oz.	11.25	24.00
10 oz.	13.25	27.00
12 oz.	14.75	30.00
14 oz.	17.00	33.00
16 oz.	18.50	36.00
24 oz.	26.00	40.00
28 oz.	29.00	44.00
32 oz.	31.00	48.00

*Assorted, ½ to 8 ounce, in 1 & 5 gross boxes, per gross, $6.75

Old Style Short, ¼, ½, 1, 2, 3, 4, 6, 8, 12 & 16 oz.

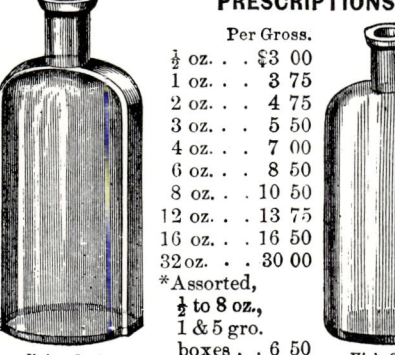
Stoppered French Square.

UNION OVAL PRESCRIPTIONS.
PLAIN HIGH OVAL PRESCRIPTIONS.

	Per Gross.
½ oz.	$3 00
1 oz.	3 75
2 oz.	4 75
3 oz.	5 50
4 oz.	7 00
6 oz.	8 50
8 oz.	10 50
12 oz.	13 75
16 oz.	16 50
32 oz.	30 00

*Assorted, ½ to 8 oz., 1 & 5 gro. boxes . . 6 50

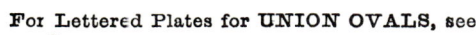
Union Oval.   High Oval.

For Lettered Plates for UNION OVALS, see page 9.

French Square, Wide Mouth.

WIDE MOUTH
FRENCH SQUARES.
FOR PILLS.

	Per Gross
½ oz.	$3 50
1 oz.	4 25
1½ oz.	
2 oz.	} 5 50
3 oz.	6 25
4 oz.	8 00
6 oz.	9 75
8 oz.	12 00
10 oz.	14 00
12 oz.	15 50
16 oz.	20 00
20 oz.	25 00

WITH EXTRA WIDTH OF MOUTH.

2 oz.	$ 5.50
7½ oz.	12.00
15 oz.	20.00

BLAKES OR OBLONGS.
ENGLISH OR TALL BLAKES.

Blake.

Tall Blake.

BLAKES.	TALL BLAKES.	Per gross. For Corks. Stoppered.
1½ drachm		$3.25 $10.25
½ oz.		3.25 10.25
1 oz.	1 oz.	4.25 11.25
2 oz.	2 oz.	5.25 12.75
3 oz.	3 oz.	6.00 15.25
4 oz.	4 oz.	7.75 17.50
6 oz.	6 oz.	9.50 20.50
8 oz.	8 oz.	11.75 24.50
10 oz.	10 oz.	14.00 27.75
12 oz.		15.50 30.75
16 oz.	16 oz.	19.50 37.00

For LETTERED PLATES for the above, see page 8.

* For contents of Assorted Cases, see page 4.

ROUND PRESCRIPTIONS.

The BOSTON or TALL Style is in use by some of the first Pharmacists, and is much liked for its symmetry and neat appearance.

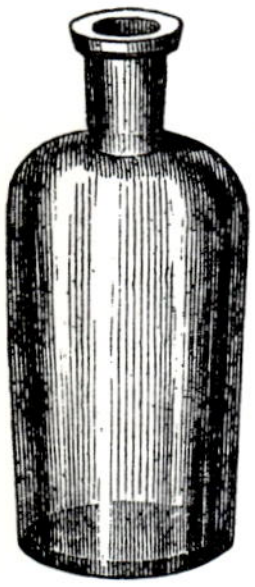

Round Shoulder.

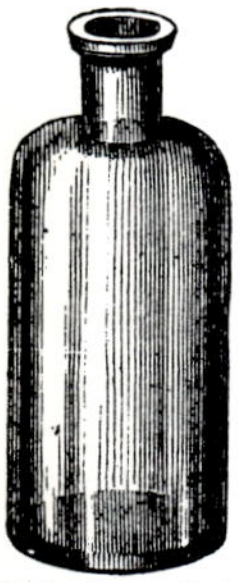

Tall or Boston Style.

NARROW MOUTH.

Plain Round Shoulder.	Boston Style, Tall, High Shoulder.	Per gross.
½ oz.	B. ½ oz.	$3 00
1 oz.	B. 1 oz.	3 75
2 oz.	B. 2 oz.	4 75
3 oz.	B. 3 oz.	5 50
4 oz.	B. 4 oz.	7 00
6 oz.	B. 6 oz.	8 50
8 oz.	B. 8 oz.	10 50
10 oz.		12 25
12 oz.	B. 12 oz.	13 75
16 oz.	B. 16 oz.	16 50
20 oz.		20 00
22 oz.		21 50
S. Quart (28 oz.)		23 50
L. Quart (32 oz.)	B. 32 oz.	28 50
Assorted ½ to 8 oz.		6 50

For Larger Sizes see SHOP FURNITURE Style.

For insertion of LETTERED PLATES see Page 9.

WIDE MOUTH.

	Per Gross.
½ oz.	$3 25
Tall ⅝ oz. 1 oz.	4 00
Tall 1¼ oz.	5 00
Tall 1½ oz. 1¾ oz. and T 1¾ oz. 2 oz. 2 oz. extra width of mouth, (No. 605)	5 25
2¼ oz. extra width of mouth, (No. 614)	5 75
3 oz. 3 oz. extra width of mouth (Quinine)	6 00
3½ oz. extra width of mouth, (No. 606)	7 25
4 oz. 4 oz., ex. width of mouth, (Reagent Style)	7 75
6 oz., extra width of mouth, (5 oz. Quinine)	8 75
6 oz.	9 25
8 oz. 8 oz. Powder	11 50
9 oz.	13 00
12 oz.	14 50
16 oz. 16 oz. Powder	19 00
20 oz.	23 00
32 oz. 32 oz. Powder	30 00

See PAINT JARS, Page 18.

STOPPERED BOTTLES.

For styles of STOPPERS see Page 6.

TINCTURES.

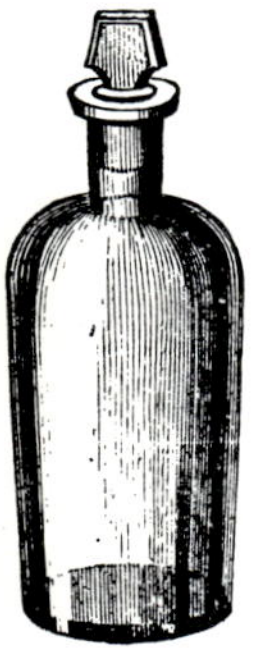

(IRON MOULD.)	Per Gross.
½ oz.	$10 25
1 oz.	10 75
1½ oz. 2 oz.	12 25
3 oz.	14 00
4 oz.	16 25
6 oz.	18 25
8 oz.	20 75
10 oz.	23 50
12 oz.	26 50
Pint	31 50
20 oz.	36 50
22 oz.	38 00
28 oz.	40 00
Quart	44 00

SALT MOUTHS.

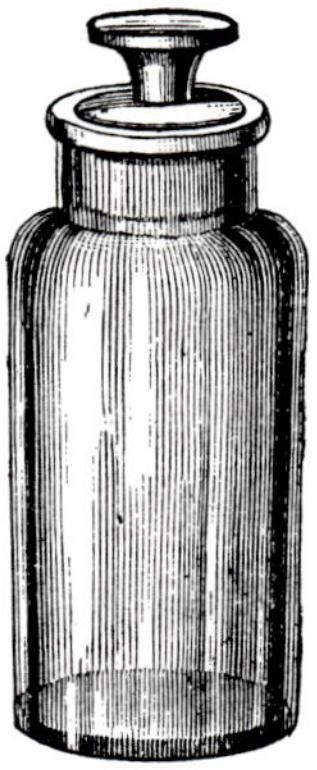

(IRON MOULD.)	Per Gross.
½ oz.	$11 00
1 oz.	12 00
1¼ oz. 1½ oz. 1¾ oz. 2 oz.	13 00
3 oz.	15 00
4 oz.	17 25
6 oz.	19 00
8 oz.	22 25
12 oz.	28 00
Pint	33 00
Quart	47 50
16 oz. Powder	33 00
32 oz. Powder	47 50

For Larger Sizes see SHOP FURNITURE LIST, Page 26.

METRIC PRESCRIPTION BOTTLES.

We have made a set of Moulds, of the popular Philadelphia Oval Pattern, adapted to dispensing Metric Prescriptions. These moulds are so constructed that they allow of the present series of lettered Prescription plates (except Blakes) being worked in them. For instance, a druggist having a 2 ounce plate can, without additional charge, have it used for making 50 cc and 60 cc bottles, or a 4 ounce plate for 125 cc bottles, as explained in the first table below. To distinguish them from the old sizes, we have, on the plain bottles, blown the Metric Content in light letters across the top of the flat side (see cut). Sample sets sent without charge on application.

We append a table showing the sizes at present furnished:

NAME.	Taking same Lettered Plate as used for	PRICE PER GROSS. For Corks.	Stoppered.
10 cubic centimeter (cc)	½ oz.	$3 00	$10 25
20 cubic centimeter (cc)	½ oz.	3 50	10 75
30 cubic centimeter (cc)	1 oz.	3 75	10 75
40 cubic centimeter (cc)	1½ oz.	4 50	12 00
50 cubic centimeter (cc)	2 oz.	4 75	12 25
60 cubic centimeter (cc)	2 oz.	5 00	12 50
100 cubic centimeter (cc)	3 oz.	6 00	14 00
125 cubic centimeter (cc)	4 oz.	7 00	16 25
150 cubic centimeter (cc)	6 oz.	8 00	17 25
200 cubic centimeter (cc)	6 oz.	9 00	19 25
250 cubic centimeter (cc)	8 oz.	10 50	20 75
300 cubic centimeter (cc)	10 oz.	12 25	24 00
350 cubic centimeter (cc)	12 oz.	13 75	26 50

The following table of Metric Equivalents may be found useful to the Pharmacist:

1 cubic centimeter or 1 milliliter	=	1 Gram of Water		1000 cubic centimeters or 1 liter	=	1000 grams or 1 kilogram.
1 cc = 16.231 minims				1 minim	=	0.062 cc
1 cc = 0.270 fluid drachm				1 fluid drachm	=	3.696 cc
1 cc = 0.034 fluid ounce				½ fluid ounce	=	14.79 cc
10 cc = 0.34 oz.				1 fluid ounce	=	29.57 cc
20 cc = 0.68 oz.				2 fluid ounces	=	59.14 cc
30 cc = 1.01 oz.				3 fluid ounces	=	88.72 cc
40 cc = 1.35 oz.				4 fluid ounces	=	118.29 cc
50 cc = 1.69 oz.				6 fluid ounces	=	177.43 cc
100 cc = 3.38 oz.				8 fluid ounces	=	236.58 cc
150 cc = 5.07 oz.				12 fluid ounces	=	354.86 cc
200 cc = 6.76 oz.				16 fluid ounces	=	473.15 cc
250 cc = 8.45 oz.				24 fluid ounces	=	709.72 cc
300 cc = 10.14 oz.				32 fluid ounces or 1 quart	=	946.30 cc or 0.9463 liter.
350 cc = 11.84 oz.						
400 cc = 13.53 oz.						
500 cc = 16.91 oz.						
1000 cc 1 liter	=	33.81 oz. 1.0567 quarts.				

BALL NECK PANELS.

	Per gross.
½ oz.	4 00
7 drachm 1 oz.	4 75
1¼ oz. and L. 1¼ oz. 1½ oz. Wide Panel 1½ oz. Narrow Panel	5 50
1¾ oz. T. 2 oz. (tall)	5 75
3 oz.	7 75
S. 4 oz. (small) B. 4 oz.	8 75
5 oz.	10 75
L. 6 oz.	13 00
L. 8 oz.	17 00

For LETTERED PLATES see Page 9.

FLAVORING EXTRACT BOTTLES.

Sides Plain. Panels on the Edges.

2 oz. for Lettered Plates	$5 25
4 oz. for Lettered Plates	7 75

SHORT FLUTED. WIDE MOUTH.

	Per gross.
¼ oz. . . L. and S.	$3 25
½ oz.	3 25
1 oz.	4 00
2 oz.	5 25

TOOTH POWDER. EXTRA WIDTH OF MOUTH.

	Per gross.
2 oz. round wide mouth (No. 605)	$5 25
2¼ oz. round wide mouth (No. 614)	5 75
3½ oz. round wide mouth (No. 606)	7 25
3 oz. round wide mouth, Flat Hood Stopper	15 00

For Tooth Powder Boxes see Page 25.

For Tooth Powder Sprinklers see Page 22.

SADDLE-BAG VIALS.

	Per gross.
T. ¾ oz. oblong, stoppered	$11 00
T. 1½ oz. oblong, stoppered	12 50

MUCILAGE.

N. Y. Style.

	Per gross.
2¼ oz. Cone 3 oz. Cone 3 oz. N.Y.	$5 50
8 oz. Cone	12 50
8 oz. Flat	16 00
Brushes and Caps	6 00

Cone Style.

INDELIBLE INKS.

1 drachm	$2 75

PANELS.

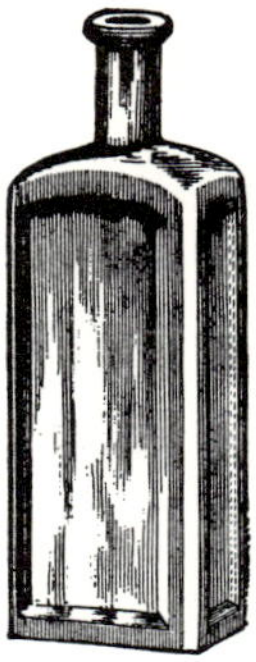

	Per gross.
½ oz.	$3 50
T. 6 drachm (tall) 1 oz.	4 00
1½ oz. 2 oz.	5 25
H. 3 oz. (high)	7 00
H. 4 oz. (high)	8 00
S. 6 oz. (small)	10 75
H. 8 oz. (high)	13 75
12 oz. (high)	21 00
16 oz.	27 00

Also any styles in the Green Glass list on page 46.

For LETTERED PLATES see Page 9.

SQUARE CARMINE INK BOTTLES.

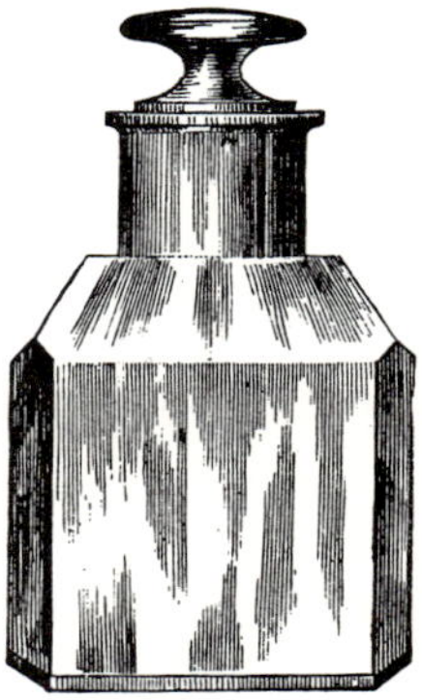

Square Carmine.

Round Shoulder or M. Carmine Ink.
¾, 1, 2, 4 and 8 ounce.

	Per gross. For Corks.	Stoppered.
½ oz.	$3 25	$9 50
1 oz.	4 00	10 25
2 oz.	5 00	12 00
4 oz.	7 75	15 00
5 oz.	9 00	17 00
8 oz.	12 00	20 00
16 oz.	19 50	37 00
1 oz. Cone Carmine	4 00	
1 oz. Round Desk Ink	4 00	

HEAVY ROUND INKS, Cut Bottoms.

½ oz. 1¾ in. Diameter, Globe Stopper	$28 00
1 oz. 2 in. Diameter, Globe Stopper	30 00
2 oz. 2¼ in. Diameter, Globe Stopper	32 00

INK WELLS.

Small	$4 50
Conical	5 00

NURSING BOTTLES.
FLINT GLASS.

  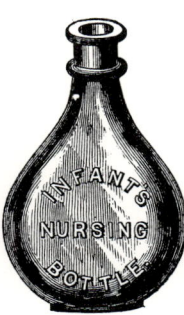 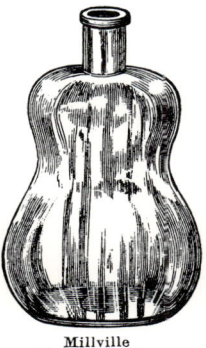 

Acme Nursing Bottle.   Empire Nursing Bottle.   Infant's Nursing Bottle.   Millville Nursing Bottle.   Baltimore Nursing Bottle, & 12 oz. Nursing Flask.

In One Gross Boxes, when so ordered.

Per gross.

ACME, Bent Neck, Round Bottom, ... $14 00

    Being without corners, this Bottle is more readily cleaned and kept sweet than any other. One side is flat as in the *Empire*. 1 Gross in Original Package.

EMPIRE, Bent Neck, ... 14 00

    The neck of the EMPIRE is bent, so that, when the Bottle is laid on its side, the contents do not reach the Stopper. It is much more convenient in feeding than the Straight Neck. 1 Gross in Original Package.

INFANT'S, Straight Neck. 1 Gross in Original Package. 12 00

MILLVILLE, No. 1, Narrow Mouth, for Rubber Nipples. 1½ Gr. Pkgs. . . ⎫
            No. 2, Wide Mouth, for the usual Rubber Fittings. 1½ Gr. Pkgs. ⎬ 12 00

BALTIMORE, Small Mouth for Rubber Nipples. 1 Gross in Original Package. 10 50

12 OUNCE NURSING FLASK, Small Mouth for Rubber Nipples. 1 Gross in Original Package 18 00

    For GREEN GLASS Nursing Bottles, see page 48.

    For Nursing Bottle Fittings, see page 54.

LETTERED NURSING BOTTLES.

    We are prepared to furnish the following style of Nursing Bottles lettered in glass with any design, at an extra cost of Five Dollars each for the lettered plate, with the usual discount on the Bottles:

    BENT NECK, ROUND BOTTOM,   (Style of the ACME.)

CASTOR OILS—FLINT.

	Per gross.
2 ounce	$5 50
4 ounce	7 75
6 ounce	9 50
8 ounce	13 00
12 ounce	17 00
16 ounce	19 50
6 ounce, Flat C. Oil	10 00

See Pages 19 & 46.

ENGLISH ESSENTIAL OILS.

	Per gross.
Extra ½ Pint	$11 50
" Pint	19 00
" Quart	32 00
" ½ Gallon	65 00

☞ We can put customers' names on the shoulders or bottoms of the ½ pint, pint and quart Essential Oils, and also on the bottom of the ½ gallon mould, at small extra cost.

For Blue, see Page 19.   For Green, see Page 48.

ENGLISH ESSENTIAL OILS.
SHOP FURNITURE STYLE.

	Per gross.
5 ounce	$16 00
10 ounce	22 00
20 ounce	31 00
40 ounce	46 00
80 ounce	80 00

In Blue Glass ten per cent. extra.

ASPIRATOR BOTTLES.
TUBULATED AT BOTTOM.

	Per Dozen.	
	For Corks.	Stoppered.
½ Pint	$6 00	$7 75
Pint	8 20	10 50
Quart	12 00	14 50
3 Pints	14 00	18 00
½ Gallon	16 00	20 00
1 Gallon	20 00	25 00
2 Gallon	30 00	36 00
3 Gallon	44 00	52 00
5 Gallon	96 00	110 00

HYACINTH GLASSES.

	Per Dozen.
White Glass	$2 50
Blue Glass	2 70
Purple Glass	2 70
Amber Glass	2 70
Assorted Glass	2 70

MISCELLANEOUS.

	Per gross.
GLYCERINE	$18 00
1 pound CALOMELS	9 50
2 ounce MORPHINE	4 50
3 ounce QUININE	6 00
5 ounce QUININE	8 75
1 ounce CHLORAL stoppered	11 50
1 pound CHLOROFORM (12 ounce, Round)	13 75
1 pound CHLOROFORM, Glass stoppered	26 50
1 drachm VIALS	3 00
2½ ounce SEWING MACHINE OIL	7 75
1¼ and 1½ ounce FLAT OCTAGON	4 75
3 ounce FLAT OCTAGON	6 00
12 ounce Lettered CITRATE MAGNESIA	16 00
BARREL MUSTARDS	9 25
WET MUSTARDS, Fancy round	10 50
WEDGE PANEL HONEY	18 00
Pint COD LIVER, oval	16 50
Quart MILK JAR	

BIRD BOTTLES AND CUPS.

	Per gross.
BIRD FEED Bottles, 2 mouths	$10 00
L BIRD BATH, Flint and Opaque	15 00
S BIRD BATH, Flint and Opaque	12 00
1 ounce Round SEED CUP	4 50
S. BIRD FOUNT	8 00
MOCKING BIRD BATH, Flint and Opaque	20 00

WIDE MOUTH PAINT JARS.

3 ounce German Style, S. F.	$11 00
N. Y. 4 ounce	8 00
N. Y. 8 ounce	12 00
½ Pint (no lip)	12 00

SAMPLE BOTTLES.

	Per Dozen.
2 oz. long OIL SAMPLE	$ 90
4 oz. long OIL SAMPLE	1 00
8 oz. long OIL SAMPLE	1 35
"BUNG THIEVES,"	20 00
MOLASSES SAMPLE	1 50
MOLASSES SAMPLES on foot	2 00

DENTISTS' SPITTOON FUNNELS.

	Per Dozen.
10 inches, (Purple Glass)	$14 00

Also Aspirator Tubes, Medicine Droppers, Cupping Glasses, Sponge Jars, Pessaries, Speculum Glasses, Eye Baths, Barometer Tubes, Garden Glasses, Insulators, Glass Fly Traps, &c.

BLUE WARE.

The articles here named are kept in stock. Any article, in either our Flint or Green Glass List, can be made in blue glass by special order.

We call especial attention to the brilliancy of color and exactness of finish of our Blue Glass.

Discount the same as on Flint Glass.

BOTTLES FOR POISONS.

These bottles are specially useful, not for Prescriptions, but for Liniments, and for the various poisonous articles, as Laudanum, Corrosive Sublimate, Oxalic Acid, Oil of Vitriol, &c., which are likely to be kept in the family medicine closet.

The frequent accidents in the use of POISONS have made a demand from well-appointed apothecary stores for a bottle which shall protect patients from danger of mistake both night and day—by the *touch*, as well as by *sight*,—in the use of poisonous preparations.

We have met this demand by a new line of bottles, of a *deep cobalt blue* color. The surface is also covered with sharp *diamond-shaped points*, tastefully arranged. It would not be easy to make any mistake with these bottles in use.

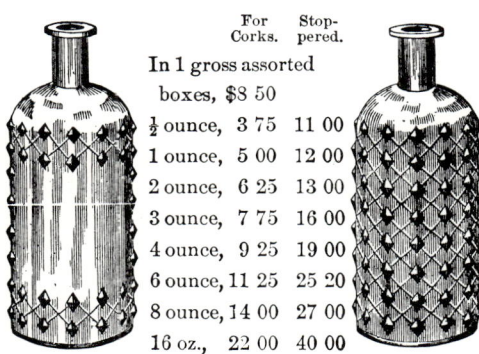

	For Corks.	Stoppered.
In 1 gross assorted boxes,	$8 50	
½ ounce,	3 75	11 00
1 ounce,	5 00	12 00
2 ounce,	6 25	13 00
3 ounce,	7 75	16 00
4 ounce,	9 25	19 00
6 ounce,	11 25	25 20
8 ounce,	14 00	27 00
16 oz.,	22 00	40 00

The same Discount as on Flint Glass.

MISCELLANEOUS.

CHLORODYNE, (L. ½ ounce F. P. L.), BLUE . 3 25
5 ounce GRANULATED CITRATE, BLUE . . . 10 00
CITRATE MAGNESIA, 12 ounce, BLUE . . . 15 00
16 ounce FRENCH SQR. Pres., Short, BLUE . 16 00

For BLUE SHOP FURNITURE see Page 27.

ENGLISH BLUE CASTOR OILS.

	Per gross.
L. 2 ounce	$6 75
L. 2½ ounce	8 00
L. 4 ounce	9 00
L. 6 ounce	10 75
8 ounce	15 00
12 ounce	19 00
16 ounce	21 00
19 ounce	23 00

BLUE PRESCRIPTIONS.

	ROUND.		FRENCH SQUARE.	
	Per Gross.		Per Gross.	
	Narrow Mouth.	Wide Mouth.	Narrow Mouth.	Wide Mouth.
½ ounce	$3 50	$4 00	$3 75	$4 25
1 ounce	4 50	5 00	4 75	5 25
2 ounce	5 75	6 25	6 00	6 50
3 ounce	6 75	7 25	7 00	7 50
4 ounce	8 25	9 25	8 50	9 50
6 ounce	10 00	11 00	10 50	11 25
8 ounce	11 00	12 00	11 75	12 50
12 ounce	12 25	13 25	13 25	14 00
16 ounce	13 50	14 50	15 50	17 00
24 ounce	17 50	18 50	20 00	
32 ounce	22 00	23 00	24 50	

ENGLISH ESSENTIAL OILS. BLUE.
EXTRA SELTZERS, HIGH SHAPE. BLUE.

	Per gross.
¼ Pint	$ 8 00
½ Pint	11 50
Pint	16 60
Quart	26 60
½ Gallon	50 00

☞ We can put customers' names on the shoulders or bottoms of the ½ pint, pint and quart Essential Oils, and also on the bottom of the ½ gallon mould, at small extra cost.

For FLINT ESSENTIAL OILS see Page 18, and for GREEN GLASS, Page 48.

PERFUMERS' WARE.

In ordering, specify in all cases whether Stoppered or for Corks. If Stoppered, note the Style of Stopper. See Page 6.

We are devoting especial attention to this line of our business, and are constantly adding to our list the best French, and also original designs. Our Stoppered Ware has obtained the commendation and custom of all the large perfumers in the United States, on account of the reliability of our stoppering, and the careful distribution of the glass around the sides and shoulders, instead of accumulating it at the bottom. Every stoppered bottle is carefully tested before packing.

When requested by Perfumers, we send, at a nominal price, boxes containing lines of our samples, marked with figures corresponding to our list, so as to insure accuracy in filling orders.

SPRINKLERS. The prices in Cork column are for the bottles unfitted. Prices in Stoppered column are for bottles fitted with metallic sprinkle tops.

416. 401. 414, 415 & 485. 421 & 422. 410, 411 & 412. 409.

PERFUMERS' EXTRACTS, &c.
Subject to discount.

No.		Per gross. For Corks.	Stop- pered.
401.	1 oz. Plain LUBIN, 3¼ in. high,	$5 00	$12 00
402.	1 oz. Plain LUBIN, 3 in. high,	5 00	12 00
403.	½ oz. Plain LUBIN,	4 00	11 00
404.	Tall ½ oz. Plain LUBIN,	4 00	11 00
405.	¼ oz. Plain LUBIN,	3 00	10 00
	2 oz. Plain LUBIN, (See 828)	6 00	14 00
	See also 861, 862 & 863 for Lubin Moulds adapted to the insertion of Lettered Plates; and 819 and 820 for Sprinkle Top Lubin.		
406.	¼ oz. ROUND EXTRACT,	3 00	10 00
407.	⅓ oz. ROUND EXTRACT,	3 00	10 00
408.	¼ oz. OVAL COUDRAY,	3 00	10 00
	½ oz. OVAL COUDRAY, (See 484)	3 75	10 00
409.	3 drachm ROUGE SQUARE, 3 Panels,	3 50	
410.	½ oz. EXTRA HEAVY SQUARE,	3 50	10 75
411.	¾ oz. EXTRA HEAVY SQUARE,	4 00	13 50
412.	1 oz. EXTRA HEAVY SQUARE,	4 50	14 00
413.	1 drachm CHLORIDE OF GOLD,	3 00	10 00
414.	1 oz. JUG-HANDLE,		16 00
415.	2 oz. JUG-HANDLE,		17 00
	3 oz. JUG-HANDLE, (See 485)		20 00
416.	½ oz. ROUND OKIE,	3 00	

No.		Per gross. For Corks.	Stop- pered.
417.	½ oz. LONG OVAL EXTRACT,	$3 25	$10 75
418.	1 oz. LONG OVAL EXTRACT,	5 00	12 00
419.	½ oz. SHORT OVAL EXTRACT, RING,	3 75	10 50
420.	1 oz. SHORT OVAL EXTRACT, RING,	4 25	11 00
421.	2 oz. FANCY SQUARE BALL-NECK PANEL,	5 00	
422.	4 oz. FANCY SQUARE BALL-NECK PANEL,	7 50	
423.	4 oz. 3 PANELS SQUARE,	7 50	
424.	1 oz. BARREL EXTRACT, (see 479)	5 00	12 00
425.	4¾ oz. SQUARE COLOGNE,	9 00	18 00
426.	2 oz. LONG CHAMPAGNE,	5 00	
427.	½ oz. ROUND RING NECK DECANTER,	3 25	10 00
428.	¾ oz. BALL NECK DECANTER,	3 50	10 50
429.	2 oz. RISTORI,	5 25	
431.	4 oz. HEART,	8 00	
432.	1 oz. ROUND, 5 RINGS,	3 75	
433.	2 oz. ROUND, 5 RINGS,	4 75	
434.	1 oz. GOTHIC PANEL,	4 50	
435.	2 oz. GOTHIC PANEL,	5 25	
436.	4 oz. THIN OVAL, BALL-NECK,	10 50	16 00
437.	S. 1 oz. BELL EXTRACT,	6 00	13 00
438.	1 oz. PEAR EXTRACT,	4 00	11 00
439.	½ oz. CONE EXTRACT,	4 50	11 00
440.	1 oz. CONE EXTRACT,	5 00	12 00

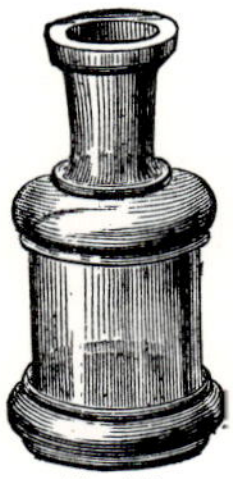
445—482.

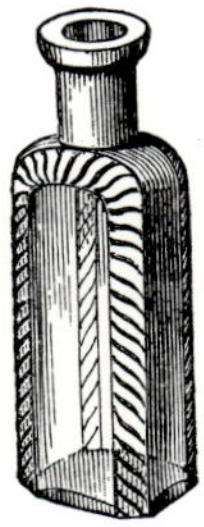
441—488.

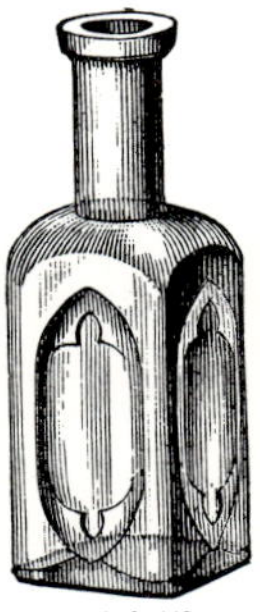
447 & 448.

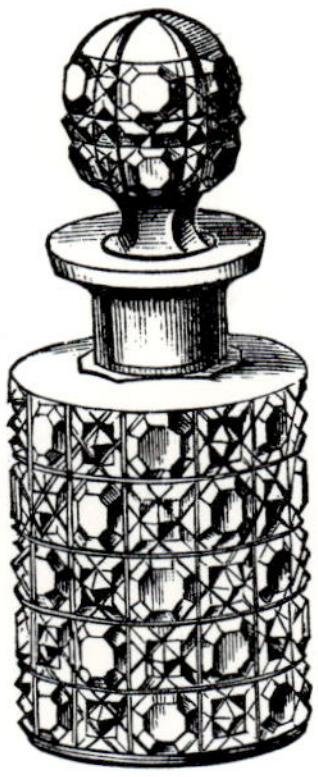
823 & 824.

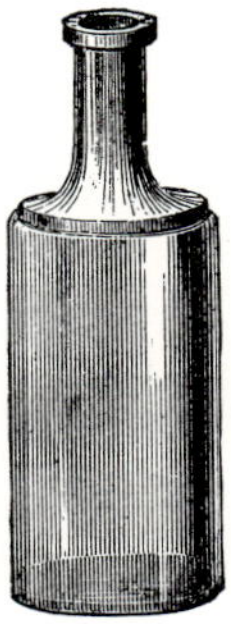
453 & 491.

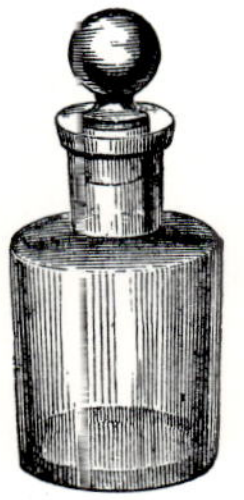
493—833.

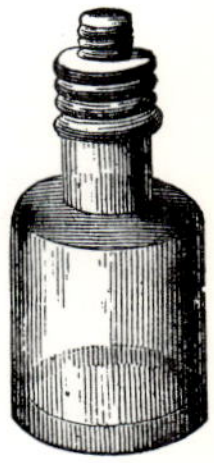
819 & 820.

No.		Per gross. For Corks.	Stoppered.
441.	½ oz. Tall Oblong Fancy,	$3 00	
442.	1 oz. Tall Oblong Fancy,	4 00	
443.	1½ oz. Tall Oblong Fancy,	4 50	
	2 oz. Tall Oblong Fancy, (See 486)	5 00	
	3 oz. Tall Oblong Fancy, (See 487)	6 50	
	4 oz. Tall Oblong Fancy, (See 488)	8 50	
444.	1 oz. Acorn,	5 00	12 00
445.	½ oz. French, 2 Rings,	4 00	11 00
446.	1 oz. French, 2 Rings,	5 00	12 00
	2 oz. French, 2 Rings, (See 851)	6 00	14
	S. 4 oz. French, 2 Rings, (See 481)	7 50	16 00
	S. 6 oz. French, 2 Rings, (See 482)	9 50	19 50
447.	Fancy Square 2 oz. Panel,	5 00	
448.	Fancy Square 4 oz. Panel,	7 50	
449.	1½ oz. Panel, Concave Edges,	5 50	
450.	1½ oz. Ball-neck Panel, Arch,	5 50	
451.	1½ oz. Tea Rose, Tall Stopper,	5 00	12 00
452.	4 oz. Urn, (Jug handle, $22)	10 00	16 00
453.	3 oz. Oval High,	6 00	13 00
	6 oz. Oval High, (See 491)	11 00	21 00
470.	4 oz. Arch Flat,	8 50	
471.	6 oz. Arch Flat,	11 50	
472.	2 oz. Thin Oval,	7 25	
473.	½ oz. Oval,	3 00	10 00
475.	1 oz. Scalloped Acorn,	5 00	12 00
476.	2 oz. Concave Square,	5 00	12 00
477.	3 oz. Thin Panel Oval, Ball-neck,	8 75	
478.	1 oz. Ball Base, Fluted Sides,	5 00	12 00
479.	½ oz. Barrel Extract, (See 424)	4 00	11 00
480.	¼ oz. French Square,	3 25	10 00
481.	S. 4 oz. French, 2 Rings,	6 00	14 00
482.	S. 6 oz. French, 2 Rings,	9 50	19 50
483.	½ oz. Blake,	3 25	10 25
	1½ drachm Blake, (See 875)	3 25	10 25
484.	½ oz. Oval Coudray,	3 75	10 00
485.	3 oz. Jug Handle,		20 00
486.	2 oz. Tall Oblong Fancy,	5 00	
487.	3 oz. Tall Oblong Fancy,	6 50	
488.	4 oz. Tall Oblong Fancy,	8 50	

No.		Per gross. For Corks.	Stoppered.
489.	½ oz. Tall French Square,	$3 25	$10 00
491.	6 oz. Oval High,	11 00	21 00
492.	3½ drachm, Night Blooming Cereus,	4 00	11 00
493.	¾ oz. Atkinson,	4 50	11 50
	1 oz. Atkinson, (See 803)	5 00	12 00
	1½ oz. Atkinson, (See 833)	5 50	12 50
494.	2 oz. Pine Apple,	6 00	13 00
495.	½ oz. Ribbed Globe,	3 50	10 00
496.	½ oz. Square Fiddle,	3 50	
497.	2 oz. Thatched Cone,	6 50	13 00
498.	2 oz. Fluted Ball-Neck Decanter,	6 00	13 00
499.	1 oz. Champagne,	4 50	11 00
800.	1½ oz Rd. Concave,	5 00	12 00
801.	2 oz. Double Oval,	5 75	
802.	2 oz. Panel Fiddle,	6 50	
803.	1 oz. Atkinson,	5 00	12 00
804.	1 oz. Flat Lubin,	5 00	12 00
805.	1 oz. Grape Decanter,	5 00	14 00
806.	1 oz. Ribbed Square,	5 00	12 50
807.	1¼ oz. Concave Square,	4 50	
808.	1½ oz. Fluted Decanter,	5 00	12 00
809.	1 oz. Satchel,	5 00	12 00
810.	¾ oz. Tassel,	5 00	12 00
811.	6 oz. Bay Rum Oil,	9 00	
812.	4 oz. B. N. Wedge Oil,	8 50	
813.	3 oz B. N. Scalloped Oval,	6 25	
814.	4 oz. Mirror Cologne.	9 50	
815.	½ oz. Diamond Cone,	4 00	
816.	2 oz. Fancy Ball-neck Panel, Plate Mould,	6 00	
817.	2 oz. Mirror Cologne,	6 25	
818.	1 oz. Clock,	5 50	
819.	¾ oz. Sprinkle Top Lubin,	5 00	12 25
820.	1 oz. Sprinkle Top Lubin,	5 50	12 75
821.	¾ oz, Oval Stand Cologne,	5 00	12 00
822.	1 oz. Ribbed Round,	4 50	11 00
823.	1 oz. Heavy Brilliant,	18 00	28 50
824.	2 oz. Heavy Brilliant,	20 00	30 00

WHITALL, TATUM & CO.

No.		Per gross. For Corks.	Stop- pered.
825.	1 oz. Beaded Ext., ...	$4 50	$11 50
826.	Tall ¼ oz. French Square, ...	3 25	10 00
827.	2 oz. Gothic Ball Neck Panel, ...	6 00	
828.	2 oz. Plain Lubin, ...	6 00	14 00
829.	1½ oz. Champagne Cologne,	4 75	
	½ oz. Champagne Cologne, (see 832) ⎱ Dark	3 25	
	1 oz. Champagne Cologne, (see 877 ⎰ Green	4 00	
	4 oz. Champagne Cologne (see 853) ⎱ or		
	S. ½ Pint Hock, (see 873) . . . ⎰ Flint.	8 50	
		10 00	
830.	1½ oz. Tooth Powder Sprinkle Top, . .	6 00	13 00
831.	3 oz. Tooth Powder Sprinkle Top, . . .	7 00	14 00
	(1½ oz. liquid equals one ounce Tooth Powder.)		
	1½ oz. Cone T. Powder, Sp. Top, (see 843).		14 00
	2 oz. Cone T. Powder Sp. Top, (see 844) .		15 00
	1½ oz. Fluted T. Powder Sp. Top, (see 854)		14 00
	3 oz. Fluted T. Powder Sp. Top, (see 855)		15 00
	Tall 2 oz. T. Powder, Sp. Top, (see 883) .		13 00
	For Tooth Powder Boxes see page 25.		
	For Tooth Powder Bottles see also 605, 606, 614, 645, 646, 902 and 903.		
832.	½ oz. Champagne Cologne, ...	3 25	
833.	1½ oz. Atkinson, ...	5 50	12 50
836.	1 oz. Oval Panel Cologne, ...	5 00	12 00
	836 takes Lettered Plates.		
837.	1 oz. Straight, Jug Handle, ...		18 00
838.	2 oz. Straight, Jug Handle, ...		20 00
839.	1 oz. Vase, Jug Handle, ...		18 00

No.		Per gross. For Corks.	Stop- pered.
840.	2 oz. Vase, Jug Handle, ...		$20 00
841.	1 oz. Vase, Double Handle, ...		22 00
842.	2 oz. Vase, Double Handle, ...		26 00
843.	1½ oz. Cone T. Powder, Sp. Top, ...		14 00
844.	3 oz. Cone, T. Powder, Sp. Top, ...		15 00
846.	1 oz. Rounded Square Sprinkle Top, . .	5 00	13 00
847.	¾ oz. Diamond Blake, (heavy).	6 75	14 00
	½ oz. Diamond Blake, (heavy), (see 878) .	5 50	12 50
848.	1 oz. Fancy Rhombus, (heavy), ...	6 75	14 00
	½ oz. Fancy Rhombus, (heavy), (see 879), .	5 50	12 50
849.	1 oz. Star Oval, ...	6 75	14 00
850.	2 oz. Hand, ...	6 50	
851.	1 oz. French, 2 Rings, ...	6 00	14 00
852.	2 oz. Monument, ...	7 50	
853.	4 oz. Champagne Cologne, ...	8 50	
854.	1½ oz. or Fluted T. Powder Sp. Top, . .		14 00
855.	3 oz. Fluted T. Powder, Sp. Top, . . .		15 00
856.	1 oz. Foot Fluted, ...	5 00	12 00
857.	2 oz. Foot Fluted, ...	7 00	14 50
858.	1 oz. Flask, ...	4 50	11 50
859.	S. 1 oz. Octagon Fluted, Tall Hex. Stop.,	8 00	22 00
860.	S. 2 oz. Octagon Fluted, Tall Hex. Stop.,	10 00	24 00
	S. 4 oz. Fluted, Tall Hex. Stop., (see 880)	18 00	36 00
	859, 860, 876, 880 and 832 Imitation of Cut Ware, very heavy.		
861.	1 oz. Panel Lubin, Plate Mould, . . .	5 00	12 00
862.	½ oz. Panel Lubin, Plate Mould, . . .	4 00	11 00
863.	2 oz. Panel Lubin Plate Mould, ...	6 00	14 00

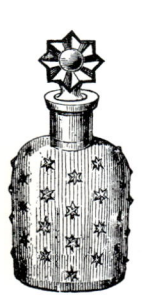      

PERFUMERS' WARE.

 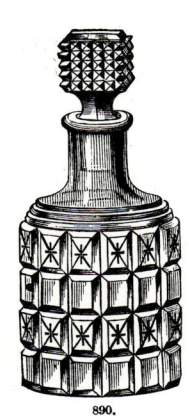   

900. **890.** **882.** **881.** **902 & 903**

No.		Per gross. For Corks.	Stop- pered.
861, 862 & 863 are adapted to the insertion of Lettered Plates. For Plain Lubins, ¼ to 2 oz., see 401, &c.			
864.	1 oz. Round, Hollow Globe St., very heavy,	22 00	
865.	2 oz. Round, Hollow Globe St., very heavy,	24 00	
867.	1 oz. Wheat Sheaf,	5 00	12 00
868.	2 oz. Wheat Sheaf,	6 00	13 00
869.	4 oz. Wheat Sheaf,	8 00	15 00
870.	5 drachm Slipper,	4 50	
871.	1 oz. Rose,	5 00	12 00
872.	1 oz. Flower,	5 00	12 00
873.	S. ½ Pint Hock. See after 829,		
874.	1¼ oz. Manilla Oil,	4 50	
	1 oz. Manilla Oil, (see 887),	4 25	
875.	1½ drachm Blake,	3 25	10 25
876.	¼ pint Cone, "Argus Eye,"	15 00	30 00
877.	1 oz. Champagne Cologne,	4 00	
878.	½ oz. Diamond Blake, (heavy)	5 50	12 50
879.	½ oz. Fancy Rhombus, (heavy)	5 50	12 50
880.	S. 4 oz. Fluted, Tall Hex. Stopper,	18 00	36 00
881.	2 oz. Cone Brilliant,	20 00	30 00
882.	S. ½ pint Thatched Cone, (very heavy),	50 00	72 00
882.	S. ½ pt. Thatched Cone, cut Lapidary St.,	84 00	
883.	Tall 2 oz. Tooth Powder Sprinkle Top,		13 00

No.		Per gross. For Corks.	Stop- pered.
885.	¾ oz. Diamond Oval,	$4 00	
886.	Tall Round 1 oz. Panel Cologne,	5 00	
886 takes Lettered Plates.			
887.	1 oz. Manilla Oil,	4 25	
888.	1 oz. Fluted Cone, B. Flut'd (Jug h. $19.25)	6 25	13 25
889.	1 oz. Cone, 3 Panels,	5 25	12 00
889 takes Lettered Plate.			
890.	2 oz. Oval Brilliant,	20 00	30 00
892.	1 oz. Cone Heavy Base, heavy,	6 00	13 00
894.	1 oz. Inverted Stopper, (Jug handle, $18)	5 00	12 00
895.	1 oz. Taper Diamond Band, heavy,	6 25	13 25
896.	2 oz. Caswell Cologne,	6 00	14 00
897.	2 oz. Panel Caswell Cologne,	6 00	14 00
897 takes Lettered Plates.			
898.	½ oz. Arequipa,	4 50	
899.	1 oz. Arequipa,	5 00	
900.	1 oz. Bell Cone Cologne, Sprinkle Top,	5 50	14 00
901.	S. 1 oz. Ring Cone, Sprinkle Top,	5 50	14 00
902.	1½ oz. Oblong T. Powder Sp. Top,		20 00
903.	3 oz. Oblong T. Powder, Sp. Top,		22 00
For Sprinkle Top Caps See Page 62.			

For ½—1 and 2 ounce Lubin, Hollow Globe Stopper, and Engraved, see page 68.

For 881, 882 and 890 Cut, see page 68.

The following are adjusted for the insertion of lettered plates: **816, 836, 861, 862, 863, 886 889, 902 and 903.**

COLOGNES.

SUBJECT TO DISCOUNT.

For Cut and Engraved Styles see pages 68 and 69.

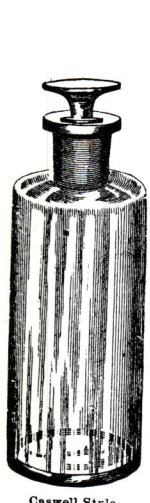
Caswell Style.

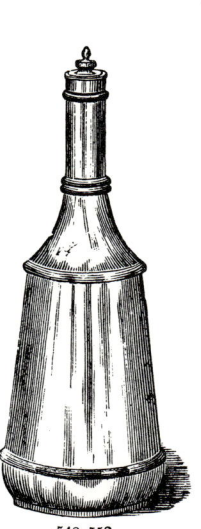
548–552.

562, 563.

555.

556.

We call special attention to our popular *Caswell* and *Burnett* styles of Colognes, the elegant finish and careful stoppering of which give great satisfaction.

For Stoppers see page 6.

No.		Per Dozen.	
		For Corks.	Stoppered.
507.	S. Pint, ROUND BURNETT STYLE, Content 12 oz.	$1 50	$2 75
	½ Pt. ROUND BURNETT, Cont. 6 oz. (see 539)	1 25	2 00

For 523-528. STOPPERED FR. SQ., 4 to 32 oz., see Page 13.
For 529-532. STOPPERED BLAKES, 4 to 16 oz., see Page 13.

No.		Per Dozen.	
		For Corks.	Stoppered.
533.	Pint SHIELD RECESS, CASWELL STYLE, . .		3 50
	Pint CASWELL, content 15 oz., (see 543) .	2 00	3 00
	½ Pt. Rd., OVAL RECESS, CASWELL (see 540)	2 00	2 60
	½ Pt. CASWELL, content 8 oz. (see 541) . .	1 25	2 25
	¼ Pt. CASWELL, (see 545)	1 00	1 50
538.	Pint COLOGNE, 3 LARGE AND 1 SMALL RING, .	2 60	3 50
539.	½ Pt. Round BURNETT, content 6 oz., . .	1 25	2 00
540.	½ Pt. CASWELL, OVAL RECESS, ...	2 00	2 60
541.	½ Pt. CASWELL, content 8 oz., ...	1 25	2 25
542.	Short ½ Pint OVAL RECESS, ...	2 00	2 60
543.	Pint CASWELL, content 15 oz., ...	2 00	3 00
544.	6 oz. ROUND COLOGNE, BALL NECK, . . .	1 25	2 00
545.	¼ Pint CASWELL, ...	1 00	1 50
546.	QUART ROUND CASWELL, ...	2 75	4 00

NEW COLOGNES.

		Per Gross.	
	With Sprinkle Tops.	For Corks.	Stoppered.
548.	1 oz., ... 14 00	5 50	14 00
549.	2 oz., ... 15 00	6 50	15 00
550.	4 oz., ... 17 00	7 75	17 00
551.	8 oz., ... 23 00	12 00	23 00
552.	16 oz., ... ; . . . 33 00	20 00	33 00

See **900.** 1 oz., Bell Cologne, a little less content than 548
See **901.** 1 oz., Ring Cone. See page 23.

	Per Doz.	
With Glass Labels, see Page 69.	For Corks.	Stoppered.
553. L. ½ Pint POMEGRANATE Pattern	3 00	4 00
554. L. ½ Pint CONE DIAMOND BRILLIANT, . .	3 00	4 00
555. L. ½ Pint FLUTED BASE AND SHOULDER, Fancy Stopper, not engraved, . . .	3 00	4 00
556. ¼ Pint DIAMOND COLOGNE, ...	5 00	6 00
557. ½ Pt. (S. Furniture Style) RD. SHOULDER TALL. Very heavy, ...	3 50	4 50
558. Pint (S. Furniture Style) RD. SHOULDER TALL. Very heavy, ...	4 50	5 50
559. TALL ½ PINT S. F. Style, Hollow Cut Stopper, .	3 50	5 00
560. TALL PINT S. F. Style, Hollow Cut Stopper, .	4 50	6 00
561. TALL QUART S. F. Style, Hollow Cut Stopper, .	7 00	9 00
562. 5 oz. CONE, not engraved,	3 00	4 00
563. 10 oz. CONE, not engraved,	4 00	5 00
564. ¼ Pt. EGG-SHAPE on Foot,	5 50	6 50
565. ½ Pt. EGG-SHAPE on Foot,	6 50	7 50
566. 5 oz. HEAVY SQUARE, .	2 50	3 50
567. 10 oz. HEAVY SQUARE, .	5 00	6 00
568. BARBER'S 18 oz. Bottle. See page 69.		
573. S. ½ Pt. OCT. MONUMENT.		
574. S. ¼ Pt. ROUND EXTRACT,	$2.00	
575. S. ½ Pt. CONE, FLUTED, "COLOGNE."		
581. DIAMOND GLOBE, FANCY STOPPER.		

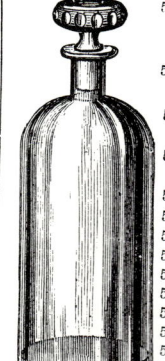
559, 560, 661.

POMADES AND GLASS BOXES.

SUBJECT TO DISCOUNT.

POMADES.

		Per Gross.
601.	1 oz. Fancy Pomade,	$4 75
602.	1 oz. Plain Oval,	4 50
603.	2 oz. Plain Oval,	5 25
604.	4 oz. Plain Oval,	7 75
605.	2 oz. Plain Round,	5 25
606.	3½ oz. Round (Ursine),	7 25
607.	1½ oz. Fancy Round	5 25
608.	2½ oz. Fancy Round	7 00
609.	1½ oz. Cone Fluted	5 25
610.	2½ oz. Cone Fluted	7 00
611.	3½ oz. Fancy Round	8 00
612.	1 oz. Fancy Oval.	4 75
613.	2 oz. Flat Oval	5 50
614.	2¼ oz. Round	5 75
615.	1½ oz. Round, Glass Lid	16 00

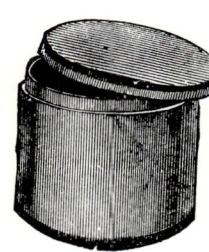

634

634.	4 oz. Round, Plain Glass Lid, Ground on	24 00
616.	1 oz. Round,	4 50
617.	3 oz. Wedge Pomade,	7 00
618.	2 oz. Spiral Pomade, Round,	5 75
919.	1½ oz. Round, Swell Side,	4 75

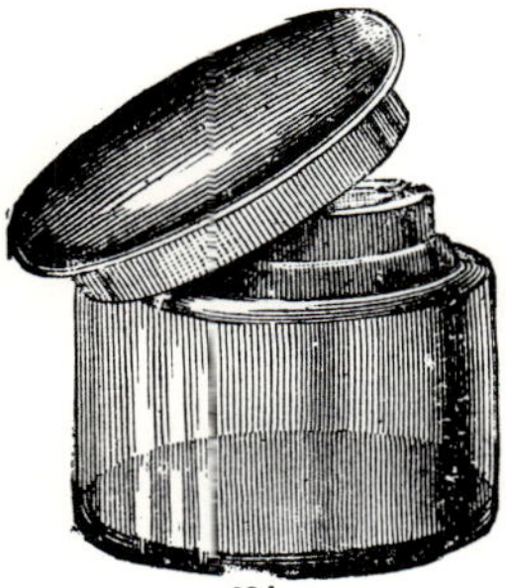

PATCH BOXES, Glass Lids.

In Flint, Dark Green, Amber and Blue Glass.

(In Opal 20 per cent. extra.)

These are preferred to earthen Ointment Jars, as grease cannot penetrate them.

		Per Gross.
620.	½ oz.,	14 00
621.	1 oz.,	15 00
622.	2 oz.,	18 00
623.	4 oz.,	21 00
624.	8 oz.,	26 00
625.	16 oz.,	33 00
621½.	1 oz. (Inside Flanges to Lid),	15 00

Oblong Opal Box.
633

OPAL BOXES.

633.	¾ oz. Oblong Box, Opal,	22 00

OINTMENT POTS.

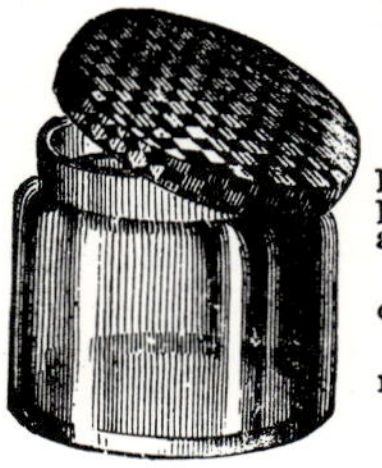

In Flint, Dark Green, Amber and Blue Glass.

(In Opal 20 per cent. extra.)

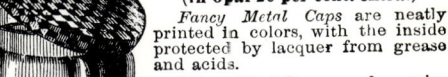

Fancy Metal Caps are neatly printed in colors, with the inside protected by lacquer from grease and acids.

White Metal Caps are of superior quality of white metal.

Jet Caps are of French Jet Enamel, lined with cork.

Per Gross.

Caps of	Fancy Metal.	White Metal.	French Jet.
625½. ¼ oz.	$8 00	$10 00	$10 00
626. ½ oz.	9 00	11 00	11 00
627. 1 oz.	11 00	13 00	13 00
628. 2 oz.	13 00	15 00	15 00
630. 4 oz.	16 00	18 00	

COLD CREAM, &c.—OPAL.

Plain, or with Sunk Letters in Red.

We can make extra lettered tops to these moulds and furnish any style of raised letters; or sunken lettering in colors.

Per Gross.

631.	½ oz. Lettered Cold Cream,	18 00
632.	1 oz. Lettered Cold Cream,	20 00
631½.	½ oz. Unlettered,	16 00
632½.	1 oz. Unlettered,	18 00

GALLIPOTS.—OPAL.

Fancy Metal Caps are neatly printed in colors, with the inside lacquered to protect the metal from grease and acids.

White Metal Caps are of superior quality of white metal.

Jet Caps are French Jet Enamel on the inside edges, lined with cork.

Per Gross.

Caps of	Fancy Metal.	White Metal.	French Jet.
633½. ¼ oz.	$10 00	$12 00	$12 00
635. ½ oz.	11 00	13 00	13 00
636. 1 oz.	13 00	15 00	15 00
637. 2 oz.	15 00	17 00	17 00
638. 3 oz.	18 00	20 00	
639. 4 oz.	20 00	22 00	

OINTMENT or TOOTH POWDER BOXES.

(Suitable also for Cold Cream.)

FLINT AND OPAL,

In quantities, made of any other color to order.

Lettered Lid Moulds can be made at ten dollars each, and the lids furnished with raised letters; or sunken and filled with color—a very neat style.

Per Gross.

		Flint.	Opal.
640.	½ oz.,	14 00	16 00
641.	1 oz.,	15 00	18 00
642.	2 oz.,	18 00	20 00
645.	1½ oz., Round Tooth Powder,	5 00	
646.	3 oz., Round Tooth Powder,	7 00	

With Sprinkler, see page 63.

DRUGGISTS, CHEMISTS and CONFECTIONERS SHOP FURNITURE.

We call special attention to the smooth stoppers, and accurate and reliable stoppering of our **Shop Furniture** ware, which have obtained for it the preference in these respects.

The bottles described below are made in moulds, thereby securing great uniformity in regard to size and height. They are more smooth than the bottles formerly made, and more brilliant in appearance.

Where requested by dealers, we send at a nominal price boxes containing lines of samples.

*** It is important, in ordering this ware, to mark the items **S. F.** (or Shop Furniture), to distinguish it from the general line of *Iron Mould* Tinctures, Saltmouths, &c., described on page 14.

X WARE.

IRON MOULD made with special care and nicety.

WITH SMOOTH BOTTOMS.

This ware is easily grasped by the hand, being tall and small in circumference.

TINCTURE BOTTLES.

	Per Dozen. For Corks.	Per Dozen. Stoppered.
Pint, height $8\frac{5}{8}$ in.	$1 75	$2 65
Quart, height $11\frac{1}{4}$ in.	3 15	3 65

SALTMOUTH BOTTLES.

	Per Dozen. For Corks.	Per Dozen. Stoppered.
Pint, height $8\frac{3}{8}$ in.	$2 10	$2 75
Quart, height $10\frac{3}{4}$ in.	3 35	4 00

XX WARE.

WOODEN MOULD. Superior Surface and free from Mould Mark.

CUT OR PUNTED BOTTOMS 10 PER CENT. EXTRA. IF VERY HEAVY AND PUNTED 40 PER CENT. EXTRA.

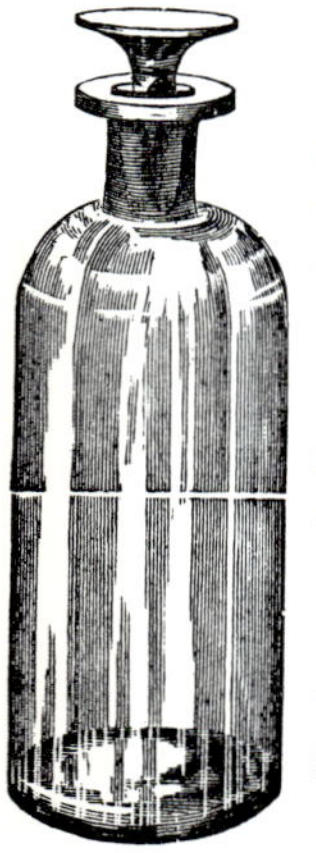

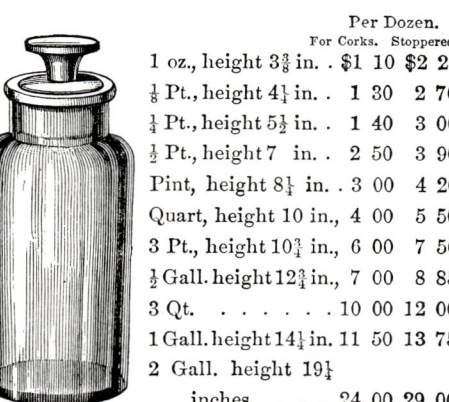

TINCTURE BOTTLES.

	Per Dozen. For Corks.	Per Dozen. Stoppered.
1 oz., height 4 in.	$1 00	$2 00
$\frac{1}{8}$ Pint, height $4\frac{1}{2}$ in.	1 10	2 25
$\frac{1}{4}$ Pint, height $5\frac{5}{8}$ in.	1 20	2 65
6 oz., height $6\frac{7}{8}$ in.	1 60	2 90
$\frac{1}{2}$ Pint, height $7\frac{1}{4}$ in.	2 00	3 10
Pint, height $8\frac{3}{4}$ in	2 50	3 55
Quart, height $10\frac{1}{2}$ in.	3 50	5 00
3 Pint, height $11\frac{1}{2}$ in.	5 00	6 20
$\frac{1}{2}$ Gall. height $13\frac{1}{4}$ in.	6 00	7 20
1 Gall. height 15 in.	9 25	10 65
2 Gallon, height $19\frac{1}{4}$ inches	22 00	25 00

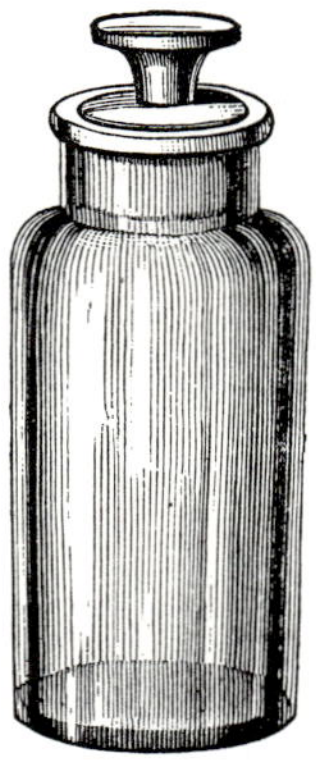

SALTMOUTH BOTTLES.

	Per Dozen. For Corks.	Per Dozen. Stoppered.
1 oz., height $3\frac{3}{8}$ in.	$1 10	$2 25
$\frac{1}{8}$ Pt., height $4\frac{1}{4}$ in.	1 30	2 70
$\frac{1}{4}$ Pt., height $5\frac{1}{2}$ in.	1 40	3 00
$\frac{1}{2}$ Pt., height 7 in.	2 50	3 90
Pint, height $8\frac{1}{4}$ in.	3 00	4 20
Quart, height 10 in.	4 00	5 50
3 Pt., height $10\frac{3}{4}$ in.	6 00	7 50
$\frac{1}{2}$ Gall. height $12\frac{3}{4}$ in.	7 00	8 85
3 Qt.	10 00	12 00
1 Gall. height $14\frac{1}{4}$ in.	11 50	13 75
2 Gall. height $19\frac{1}{4}$ inches	24 00	29 00

XXX WARE.

Extra Weight and Quality. Punted. Hollow, Flat, Cut Stopper.

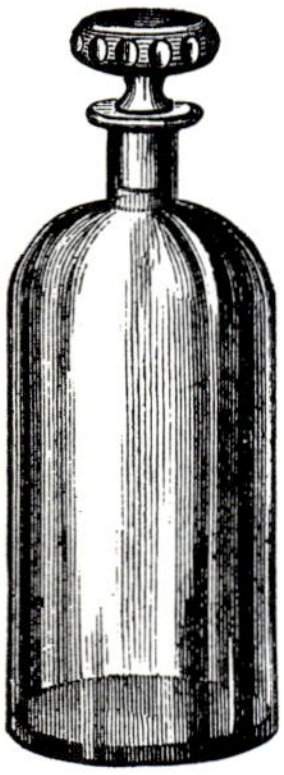

TINCTURE BOTTLES.

With Round Shoulders.

	Per Dozen. Stoppered.
$\frac{1}{8}$ Pint, height $4\frac{3}{8}$ in.	$3 75
$\frac{1}{4}$ Pint, height 6 in.	4 25
$\frac{1}{2}$ Pint, height $7\frac{3}{4}$ in.	5 50
Pint, height $9\frac{1}{4}$ in.	6 50
Quart, height 11 in.	8 00
$\frac{1}{2}$ Gallon, height 14 in.	12 00
1 Gall., height $15\frac{3}{4}$ in.	17 50
2 Gall., height 20 in.	43 00

SALTMOUTH BOTTLES.

With Round Shoulders.

	Per Dozen. Stoppered.
$\frac{1}{8}$ Pint, height $4\frac{1}{2}$ inches,	$4 25
$\frac{1}{4}$ Pint, height 6 inches	4 75
$\frac{1}{2}$ Pint, height $7\frac{1}{2}$ inches	6 25
Pint, height $8\frac{3}{4}$ inches	7 25
Quart, height $10\frac{1}{2}$ inches	9 00
$\frac{1}{2}$ Gal., height $13\frac{1}{2}$ inches	14 00
1 Gal., height $15\frac{1}{2}$ inches	21 00
2 Gal., height 20 inches	48 00

A Variety of Other Styles in Addition to These Fac-similes of Glass Labels
SUPPLIED BY
WHITALL, TATUM & CO.
410 Race St., PHILAD'A.   46 & 48 Barclay St., N. Y.

1. PIMENTA.
2. TR. ARNICÆ.
4. VIN. XERIC.
5. OL. OLIVÆ.
7. CANTHARID.
8. P. OPII.
10. R. OPI. GAM.
13. ANTIM. NIG.
22. C. AURANT.
24. TR. CINCH.
25. P. RHEI.
27. TR. CIMICIF.

SHOP FURNITURE.

BLUE SHOP FURNITURE.
BLUE TINCTURES.

With Round shoulders and Mushroom stoppers. Per Doz.

1/16 Pint, height 4 inches,	$2 50
1/8 Pint, height 4½ inches,	2 90
¼ Pint, height 5⅝ inches,	3 30
½ Pint, height 7¼ inches,	3 50
Pint, height 8¾ inches,	4 00
Quart, height 10½ inches,	6 00
½ Gallon, height 13¼ inches,	8 00
1 Gallon, height 15 inches	14 00

BLUE SALTMOUTHS.

With Round shoulders and Mushroom stoppers. Per Doz.

1/16 Pint, height 3⅜ inches,	$2 70
1/8 Pint, height 4¼ inches,	3 25
¼ Pint, height 5½ inches,	3 65
½ Pint, height 7 inches,	4 35
Pint, height 8¼ inches,	5 35
Quart, height 10 inches,	6 60
½ Gallon, height 12¾ inches,	11 20
1 Gallon, height 14¼ inches,	17 25

SYRUP DISPENSING BOTTLES.

With Loose Stoppers. White or Blue.

	Per Doz.
½ Pint	$4 10
Pint	4 60
Quart	6 00
½ Gallon	8 00
1 Gallon	15 00

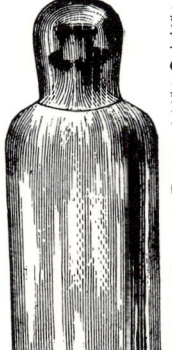
Balsam Bottle.

BALSAM OR OIL BOTTLES.

With Glass Caps.

	Per Doz.
2 ounce	$5 25
4 ounce	5 65
8 ounce	6 10
Pint	6 60
Quart	8 00
½ Gallon	12 00

Syrup Bottle.

ENGLISH BALSAM OR OIL BOTTLES.

With Ground Caps.

	Per Doz.
Pint	$10 50
Quart	13 50
½ Gallon	16 50

ETHER BOTTLES.
Used also for CHLOROFORM.

Extra Heavy, Polished Bottoms Accurately Ground Stoppers, and Ground Glass Caps.

	Per Doz.
¼ Pint	$7 50
½ Pint	8 00
Pint	10 50
Quart	13 50

Ether Bottle. 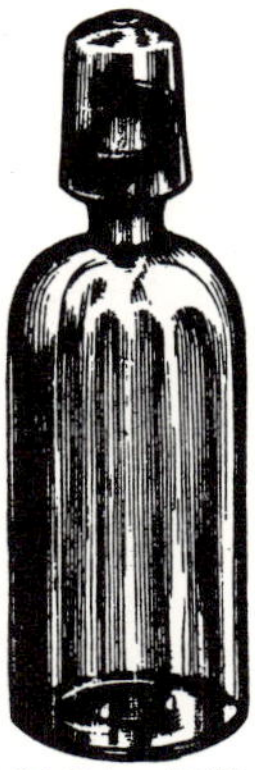   English Balsam Bottle.

For Presc. Desk Bottles, see page 28.

GLASS LABELS FOR BOTTLES.
OF OUR OWN MANUFACTURE.

In Single lines. Double lines 3 to 5 cts. each extra.

No. [ORDER BY NUMBERS.]

1. Square Label, gold ground, with black letters,
2. Square Label, white ground, with black letters, gold border,
3. Square Label, oval centre, blue, red, black or green corners, gold borders,
7. Square Label, gold letters, shaded with red, white ground, gold borders,
8. Oval Label, gold ground, with black letters,
9. Square Label, gold ground, with black letters, embossed scroll and border,
10. Square Label, white ground, with black letters, shaded with gold, gold border,
*12. Square Label, white ribbon on purple ground, gold border,
13. Oval L., white gr'nd, black letters, gold border,
14. Oval L., pink gro'nd, gold letters, gold border,
*15. Shield L., white ground, black letters, shaded with gold,
*16. Shield L., gold gr'nd, black letters, gold border,
*17. Shield Label, white ground, black letters, gold border,
*18. Shield L., pink gr'nd, gold letters, gold border,
19. Oval Label, gold ground, black letters, embossed border,
20. Oval Label, white ground, black letters, green inside of gold border,
*21. Square Label, white ribbon on green ground, gold border,
22. Square Label, gold border, white oval centre, black letters,
23. Square Label, scollop, white centre, with blue, red, black or green and gold border,
*27. Shield L., white gr'd, black letter, gold border,
*28. Shield L., white gr'nd, gold letter, gold border,
29. Oval Label, white ground, black letter, shaded with gold, gold border,
*30. Square Label, matted gold ground, black letter, bright gold border,

Those marked (*) are specially expensive.

Roman letters on any of the above styles, **extra price.** Any styles not enumerated above furnished to order **by** sending pattern or sample of style. Special styles, special prices. Gallon labels, 5 cents extra, each. 2 Gallon, 10 cents extra, each.

Please order by numbers, as it avoids mistakes, **and** give colors wanted in Nos. 3 and 23.

We furnish our Cologne Bottles labeled with

SHIELDS, OVALS AND SQUARES,
WITH OR WITHOUT HANDSOME MEDALION CENTRES.

Persons wishing to have their own names or other matter put on labels, at extra price, can do so by sending explicit orders to that effect.

GLASS LETTERED BOTTLES
FOR
PRESCRIPTION CASE.

NEW STYLE. IN THREE COLORS. Patented Mar. 25th, 1879.

We are prepared to furnish sets of bottles, 1 and 4 ounce Tinctures and 1 and 4 ounce Saltmouths, bearing IN RAISED LETTERS OF GROUND GLASS, the names of articles mostly used at the Prescription Case. The advantages of this series are:

I. The labels are blown in the glass and are as indestructible as the Bottle itself. Heat or washing will not affect them.

II. The surface of the letter is ground so as to easily impress the eye.

III. The lips of the Tincture Bottles are wide, and specially constructed for dropping.

IV. The mouths of the Saltmouths are of extra width, almost even with the side of the Bottle, and they are covered from the dust by a Hood Stopper, with top larger than lip of bottle, so as to be easily grasped.

V. The stoppering of both Tinctures and Saltmouths is done with especial care, and tested before packing.

VI. Amber Bottles are furnished for articles affected by light.

Content, 4¼ Fluid Oz., or ⅛ Liter.

VII. Poisons are in Dark Blue Bottles, with raised diamonds around the name, thus, both by **sight** and touch, guarding against accident.

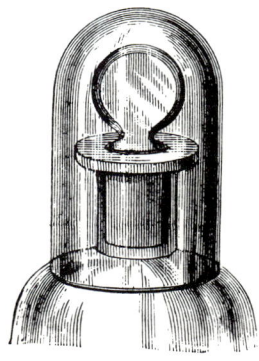

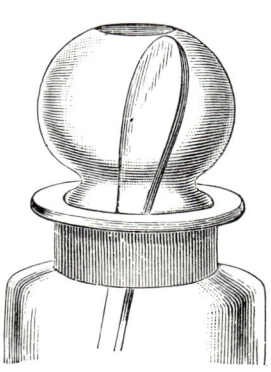

	TINCTURES.		SALTMOUTHS.	
	Per Doz.	Per Grs.	Per Doz.	Per Grs.
1 oz.,	$1 25	$12 00	$1 35	$13 00
¼ Pint,	1 75	18 50	1 93	20 50

TINCTURES with LOOSE GLASS CAPS, 60 cents per dozen extra, net.

SALTMOUTHS with HOLLOW STOPPER $1.00 per dozen extra. For use with a BONE SPOON.

See also LETTERED REAGENT and ACID BOTTLES, pages 34 and 35.

If, by constant handling, the surface of the letters becomes less clear than at first, a little chalk will restore it fully.

We have also moulds for 6, 8, 16 and 32 ounce Tinctures, in which glass names can be inserted on special order.

ACIDS.

Pint and Quart Flint Stoppered Acids, lettered ACID NITRIC, ACID SULPHURIC, ACID MURIATIC, per dozen, Pints, $3.00; Quarts, $4.00, net.

Selections can be made from the following list and ordered by numbers attached.

PRESCRIPTION CASE BOTTLES.

ALL SIZES AND STYLES FURNISHED. ENGRAVED TO ORDER OR BLANK.

4 OZ. SALTMOUTHS.
HEIGHT 4¾ INCHES.

- 3000. Acaciæ Pulv.
- 3001. Acid Citric.
- 3002. Acid Tannic.
- 3003. Acid Tartaric.
- 3004. Aloe Soc. Pulv.
- 3005. Alumen.
- 3006. Ammon. Bromid.
- 3007. Ammon. Carb.
- 3008. Ammon. Mur.
- 3009. Ant. et. Pot. Tart. (Blue.)
- 3010. Assafœtida.
- 3011. Bismuthi Subcarb.
- 3012. Bism. et. am. Citras. (Amber.)
- 3013. Bismuthi Subnit.
- 3014. Camphora.
- 3015. Chloral.
- 3016. Cinchoniæ Sulphas.
- 3017. Cinchonidiæ Sulphas. (Amber.)
- 3018. Colocynth Co. Ext.
- 3019. Cretæ Præpar.
- 3020. Digitalis Pulv. (Blue.)
- 3021. Ferri Citras.
- 3022. Ferri et. Am. Citras.
- 3023. Ferri Persulph.
- 3024. Ferri Pyrophos. (Amb.)
- 3025. Ferri et Quin. Citras. (Amber.)
- 3026. Ferri Subcarb.
- 3027. Ferri Sulphas.
- 3028. Ferri Sulph. Exsic.
- 3029. Gallæ Pulv.
- 3030. Glycyrrh. Pulv.
- 3031. Glycyrrh. Ext. Pulv.
- 3032. Hydrarg. Cum Creta.
- 3033. Hydrarg. Chlor. Cor. (Blue.)
- 3034. Hydrarg. Chlor. Mit. (Amb.)
- 3035. Hydrarg. Oxid. Rub. (Blue.)
- 3036. Iodinium.
- 3037. Ipecac. Pulv.
- 3038. Doveri Pulvis.
- 3039. Jalapæ Ext. Pulv.
- 3040. Magnesia.
- 3041. Magnesii Sulphas.
- 3042. Cretæ Pulv. Mistur.
- 3043. Opii. Pulv.
- 3044. Pepsina.
- 3045. Plumbi Acetas. (Blue.)
- 3046. Potass. Acetas.
- 3047. Potass. Bicarb.
- 3048. Potass. Bitart.
- 3049. Potass. Bromid.
- 3050. Potass. Carbonas.
- 3051. Potass. Citras.
- 3052. Potass. Chloras.
- 3053. Potass. Iodid.
- 3054. Potass. Nitras.
- 3055. Quiniæ Sulphas.
- 3056. Rhei Pulv.
- 3057. Rhei Co. Pulv.
- 3058. Sapo Alba.
- 3059. Sodii Bicarb.
- 3060. Sodii Boras.
- 3061. Sodii Bromid.
- 3062. Sodii Phosphas.
- 3063. Tragac. Pulv.
- 3064. Zinci Sulphas.
- 3065. Sacch. Lactis.
- 3066. Saccharum.
- 3067. Acid Gallic.
- 3068. Aloes Cape. Pulv.
- 3069. Aromat Pulv.
- 3070. Calc. Phosph. Precip.
- 3071. Capsici Pulv. (Blue)
- 3072. Calc. Carb. Precip.
- 3073. Cerii. Oxalas.
- 3074. Ferrum Redact.
- 3075. Ferri et Potas. Tart.
- 3076. Acid Benzoic.
- 3077. Acid Salicylic.
- 3078. Calc. Phosph. Precip.
- 3079. Cupri Sulphas. (Blue.)
- 3080. Cupri Subacetas. (Blue.)
- 3081. Dextrin.
- 3082. Potass. Permang.
- 3083. Potass. Sulphas.
- 3084. Santonine. (Amber.)
- 3085. Sodii Sulphis.
- 3086. Sodii Hyposulph.
- 3087. Sodii Iodid (Amber.)
- 3088. Sulphur Sub.
- 3089. Sulphur Precip.
- 3090. Zinci Carb. Precip.
- 3091. Zinci Oxidi.
- 3092. Jalap Rad Pulv.
- 3093. Cubebæ Pulv.
- 3094. Acacia Gran.
- 3095. Ergota (Amb.)
- 3096. Magnesii Carb.
- 3097. Sassafras Medulla.
- 3098. Zingiber Pulv.
- 3099. Oleum Theobromæ (Am.)
- 3100. Crocus.
- 3101. Aloes et Canellæ.

1 OZ. SALTMOUTHS.
HEIGHT 3⅛ INCHES.

- 3200. Argenti Nitras. (Amber.)
- 3201. Ferrum Redact.
- 3202. Piperin.
- 3203. Resina Podophyl.
- 3204. Iodoform.

4 OZ. TINCTURES,
HEIGHT 5⅛ INCHES.

- 3300. Acid. Acetic.
- 3301. Acid. Phosphor. Dilut.
- 3302. Acid. Sulphur. Arom.
- 3303. Acid. Sulphur. Dilut.
- 3304. Alcohol.
- 3305. Chloroform.
- 3306. Glycerit. Acid. Tannic.
- 3307. Liq. Potas. Arsenit.
- 3308. Mel. Despum.
- 3309. Ol. Origani.
- 3310. Ol. Sassafras.
- 3311. Spt. Ætheris Comp.
- 3312. Spt. Ammon Arom.
- 3313. Glycerina.
- 3314. Aconiti Radic. Tinct. (Blue.)
- 3315. Belladonnæ. Tinct. (Blue.)
- 3316. Digitalis. Tinct. (Blue.)
- 3317. Ferri Chloridi. Tinct.
- 3318. Nucis Vomic. Tinct. (Blue.)
- 3319. Opii. Tinct. (Blue.)
- 3320. Opii. Deodor. Tinct. (Blue)
- 3321. Verat. Virid. Tinct. (Blue.)
- 3322. Antimonii. Vinum.
- 3323. Colchici Rad. Vinum. (Blue.)
- 3324. Colchici Semen. Vinum (Blue.)

1 OZ. TINCTURES.
HEIGHT 3½ INCHES.

- 3400. Ol. Amygd. Am. Amber.
- 3401. Ol. Anisi. "
- 3402. Ol. Cari. "
- 3403. Ol. Caryoph. "
- 3404. Ol. Chenopod. "
- 3405. Ol. Copaibæ. "
- 3406. Ol. Coriandri. "
- 3407. Ol. Cubebæ. "
- 3408. Ol. Fœniculi. "
- 3409. Ol. Gaultheriæ. "
- 3410. Ol. Hedeomæ. "
- 3411. Ol. Juniperi. "
- 3412. Ol. Lavand. "
- 3413. Ol. Menth. Pip. "
- 3414. Ol. Menth. Vir. "
- 3415. Ol. Monardæ. "
- 3416. Ol. Rosmarini. "
- 3417. Ol. Succin Rect. "

S. 6 drachm.　　S. 4 drachm.　　S. 3 drachm.　　S. 2 drachm.　　S. 1 drachm.　S. ½ drachm.　S. ¼ drachm.

AN ENTIRELY NEW STYLE OF
HOMEOPATHIC VIALS.

Extra Weight, Round Mouths, Heavy Lips, "Patent Tool" Finish, and Annealed.

SPECIAL DISCOUNT.

WRAPPED IN PAPER AND PACKED IN ONE GROSS PASTE BOARD BOXES.

We call especial attention to our **HOMEOPATHIC VIALS.**

WEIGHT.—They are double the weight and thickness of glass of those often sold, and therefore less liable to break.

MOUTHS.—The mouths are formed by "Patent Tools," and are uniform in diameter, and always round.

LIPS.—The lips are thick, well shaped, regular, and strong for corking.

ANNEALING.—Our Vials are annealed under high heat after they are made, and thus are not fragile from sudden cooling in the manufacture.

In a combination of the above advantages our Homeopathic Ware stands alone in the market.

IN ORDERING PLEASE ALWAYS STATE THE STYLE DESIRED, WHETHER LONG OR SHORT.
FOR FRENCH SQUARES AMBER, SEE PAGE 13.

HOMEOPATHIC VIALS.

LONG AND SHORT HOMEOPATHIC VIALS.

Per Gross.
White.

1/8, 1/4, and 1/2 drachm	$1 12½
1 drachm	1 25
1½ and 2 drachm	1 50
3 drachm	2 00
4 drachm	3 00
6 drachm	4 00
8 drachm	5 00

AMBER AND BLUE COLORS Ten per cent. less discount from Card Price.

☞ Stoppered Homeopathic Vials $10.00 per gross additional, less same discount.

In absence of special advice, WHITE Vials will always be sent.

HOMEOPATHIC CASE VIALS.

Per Gross.

1/8, 1/4 and 1/2 drachm	$1 25
1 drachm	1 50
1½ drachm	} 1 75
2 drachm	2 50
3 drachm	3 50
4 drachm	4 50
6 drachm	6 00
8 drachm	

SPECIAL SIZES OF HOMEOPATHIC VIALS MADE ONLY TO ORDER.

S. 2 drachm.   S. 1 drachm.

In the numbers given below, the last two figures indicate the *length* in millimeters. The *diameter* is expressed in the preceding figure or figures.

Thus, 5 x 18 is 18 millimeters in length, and 5 in diameter.
12 x 50 is 50 "   "   " 12 "

SCALE OF MILLIMETERS.

10   20   30   40   50   60   70   80   90   100
  5   15   25   35   45   55   65   75   85   95

PRICES OF HOMEOPATHIC VIALS.
PER GROSS.

5x18	$1 25	10x60	$1 40	13x47	$1 40	15x63	$2 00
6x28	1 25	10x75	1 50	13x50	1 40	15x68	2 00
6x30	1 25	10x80	1 50	13x56	1 50	16x47	1 75
6x35	1 25	11x35	1 25	13x60	1 75	17x42	1 75
7x35	1 25	11x45	1 40	14x42	1 40	17x53	2 00
8x34	1 25	11x65	1 50	14x52	1 50	17x57	2 00
9x30	1 25	11x70	1 50	14x57	1 75	17x75	2 50
9x43	1 25	11x75	1 50	14x70	1 75	18x50	2 00
10x35	1 25	11x80	1 75	14x80	2 00	18x57	2 25
10x37	1 25	12x50	1 40	15x42	1 50	19x60	2 50
10x45	1 25	13x36	1 40	15x52	1 75	21x63	3 00
10x57	1 40						

MISCELLANEOUS.
Same Discount as Flint-Glass Drug Ware.

DECORATED SHOW JAR.
Per Pair.
10 Gallon, ... $60 00

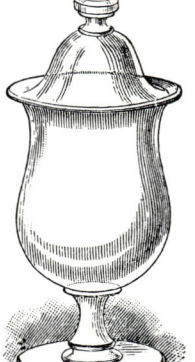

COUNTER URNS.
Per Doz.
½ Pints, ... $10 00
Pints, ... 11 00
Quarts, ... 13 00
½ Gallon, ... 22 00
Gallon, ... 31 00
1½ Gallon, ... 46 00
2 Gallon, ... 62 00

PINEAPPLE SHOW BOTTLES, PLAIN.
Each.
	3 Pieces.	4 Pieces.
Quart,	$3 00	$3 50
½ Gallon,	3 50	4 00
Gallon,	4 00	5 00
1½ Gallon,	4 50	6 00
2 Gallon,	5 00	7 00
3 Gallon,	7 00	9 00

Engraving Extra.

CYLINDER & FLAT SHOW BOTTLES.
ON FOOT—STOPPERED.
Each.
12 x 1 inch,	$1 35
15 x 1¼ inch,	1 50
13 x 1½ inch,	2 00
18 x 2 inch,	2 25
18 x 3 inch,	2 50
21 x 2 inch,	2 75
21 x 3 inch,	3 00
24 x 2½ inch,	3 75
24 x 3 inch,	4 50
30 x 2½ inch,	5 50
30 x 4 inch,	7 25
36 x 3 inch,	7 25
36 x 4 inch,	9 00

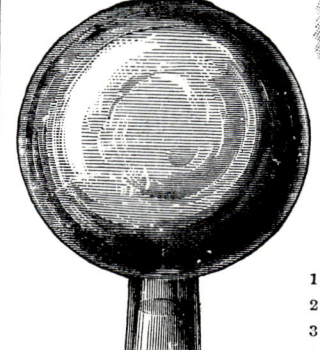

GLOBE SHOW BOTTLES.
STOPPERED.
Each.
1 Gallon,	$1 75
2 Gallon,	2 50
3 Gallon,	3 50
4 Gallon,	4 50

Decorated Show Jar.

CONFECTIONERY RING JARS.
WITH GLASS TOPS.
Per Doz.
½ Pint,	$10 00
Pint,	11 00
Quart,	12 00
½ Gallon,	15 00
Gallon,	23 50
1½ Gallon,	31 00
2 Gallon,	37 50

FISH GLOBES. With Foot.
Per Doz.
Quart,	$10 50
½ Gallon,	13 50
Gallon,	18 00
1½ Gallon,	22 00
2 Gallon,	25 00
3 Gallon,	36 00
4 Gallon,	48 00

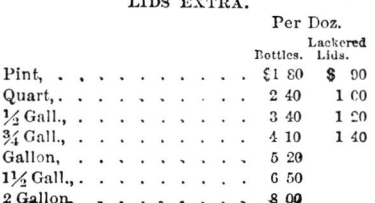

Confectionery Ring Jar.

SPECIE JARS—Short and Long.
LIDS EXTRA.
Per Doz.
	Lackered Bottles.	Lids.
Pint,	$1 80	$ 90
Quart,	2 40	1 00
½ Gall.,	3 40	1 20
¾ Gall.,	4 10	1 40
Gallon,	5 20	
1½ Gall.,	6 50	
2 Gallon,	8 00	

FISH GLOBES—Hanging.
CHAINS EXTRA.
Per Doz.
4 in. diameter, ½ Pint,	$3 75
5 in. diameter, Pint,	4 50
6 in. diameter, Quart,	5 25
7 in. diameter, ½ Gallon,	6 00
8 in. diameter, Gallon,	7 50
10 in. diameter, 2 Gallon,	11 00

AQUARIA.
Per Doz.
6 in. diameter, Quart,	$7 00
7 in. diameter, ½ Gallon,	8 00
8 in. diameter, Gallon,	10 00
10 in. diameter, 2 Gallon,	13 00
12 in. diameter, 5 Gallon,	32 00
16 in. diameter, 10 Gallon,	90 00
20 in. diameter, 12 Gallon,	125 00

CHEMICAL GLASSWARE

FOR

Laboratories,   **Colleges,**

Museums,   **Assaying Works,**

Institutes of Technology,   **Academies, &c.**

We respectfully call your attention to the Line of Chemical Glass Ware of *our own manufacture.* The desirableness of purchasing this class of goods at home, instead of depending upon the foreign sources of supply, will be manifest. By so doing the carrying of a large and expensive stock is avoided; the opportunity of effecting changes in the form of apparatus for special purposes is afforded, and promptness in filling orders greatly facilitated.

Under the advice and direction of experienced chemists, we have for a number of years been perfecting our work in these lines, and now feel confident that the character both of our glass and our workmanship will be found, for all the usual needs of the Laboratory, to compare favorably with the imported wares.

We therefore invite your attention to our **CHEMICAL CATALOGUE,** and hope by careful attention to the wants of chemists, to attain the same high rank in the manufacture of Chemical Glass Ware, as has been kindly and universally conceded to us in the line of Druggists' Glass Ware.

We would specially call your attention to our prices, and invite a comparison of them, *after deducting the discounts,* with those of the importers of foreign goods, and with the cost of actual importation, after paying all importing expenses. We would further solicit an opening order for samples of our work, in order that the above claims may be fully tested by you before placing your larger orders.

Parties so desiring can order goods by the metric system of measures and capacities.

Our Chemical Glass Ware is in use in the following, as well as other eminent Laboratories of Collegiate and Scientific Institutions:

Harvard,	University of Vermont,	Columbia,	Stevens Inst. Techn'gy,
Yale,	" Michigan,	Princeton,	Jefferson Med. College,
Brown,	" Penn'a,	Vassar,	Johns Hopkins,
Cornell,	Mass. Inst. Technology,	Wesleyan,	&c., &c.

Our Glass, being free from Lead, has the advantages of being hard and durable, light in weight, and not liable to oxidation. It is therefore well suited for organic analysis, not oxidizing with acids and alkalies, nor becoming gray with Hydric Sulphide, nor dull by boiling with water.

GLASSWARE OF ANY DESIGN MADE TO SPECIAL ORDER.

CHEMICAL REAGENT BOTTLES.
WITH GROUND GLASS LABELS. (Patented.)

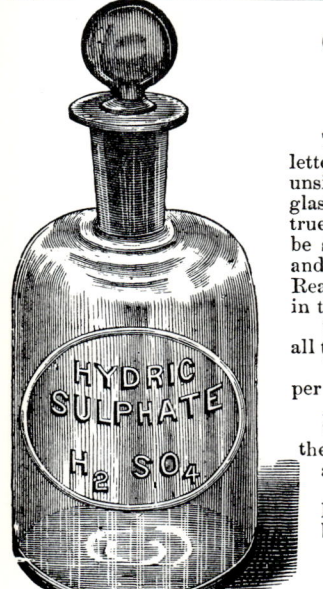

Content, 4¼ Fluid Oz., or ⅛ Liter.

These Bottles have the CHEMICAL NAMES and EQUIVALENTS in raised letters GROUND ON THE SURFACE, thus avoiding the danger of confusion and unsightly appearance of Paper Labeled Bottles. They are made from glass containing *no Lead, Zinc, or other metallic flux*, and in the points of true shape, thin dropping lip, and perfect stoppering, we believe them to be superior to the imported bottles in general use. Prominent chemists and the leading Universities express entire approval of the Lettered Reagent Bottles, and we have received large orders for Laboratories, &c., in this country and in Europe.

The great improvement which we have effected, of grinding the surfaces of all the letters and figures in the label, makes it a PERFECT REAGENT BOTTLE.

We furnish these Bottles with LOOSE GLASS CAPS (see page 28) at 60 cts. per dozen extra.

Additional moulds made for new labels with orders for a gross or more.

These REAGENT BOTTLES, having indestructible labels, allow of washing the lips free from dust or impurity with the greatest facility. The importance of this practical advantage will be manifest to every Chemist.

If by constant handling the ground surfaces of the letters become less clear than at first, a little chalk will restore them entirely. A dark background is an advantage.

1-4 PINT REAGENT BOTTLES, 1-8 LITER.

No.
1. $H_2 S$ . . . . . Hydric Sulphide, (Amber.)
2. $H Cl$ . . . . . Hydric Chloride.
3. $H C_2 H_3 O_2$ . . Hydric Acetate.
4. $H_2 SO_4$ . . . . Hydric Sulphate.
5. $H NO_3$ . . . . Hydric Nitrate.
6. $K_4 Cfy$ . . . . Potassic Ferrocyanide.
7. $K Cy S$ . . . . Potassic Sulphocyanide.
8. $K_2 CO_3$ . . . . Potassic Carbonate.
9. $K_2 SO_4$ . . . . Potassic Sulphate.
10. $K I$ . . . . . Potassic Iodide.
11. $K_3 Cfy$ . . . . Potassic Ferricyanide.
12. $K HO$ . . . . Potassic Hydrate.
13. $K_2 Cr_2 O_7$ . . . Potassic Acid Chromate.
14. $Na_2 H PO_4$ . . . Di Sodic Hydric Phosphate.
15. $N H_4 HO$ . . . Ammonic Hydrate.
16. $(N H_4)_2 S$ . . . Ammonic Sulphide, (Amber.)
17. $N H_4 Cl$ . . . . Ammonic Chloride.
18. $(N H_4)_2 CO_3$ . . Ammonic Carbonate.
19. $(N H_4)_2 C_2 O_4$ . . Ammonic Oxalate.
20. $Ba Cl_2$ . . . . . Baric Chloride.
21. $Ca Cl_2$ . . . . . Calcic Chloride.
22. $Ca SO_4$ . . . . Calcic Sulphate.
23. $Ca H_2 O_2$ . . . Calcic Hydrate.
24. $Mg SO_4$ . . . . Magnesic Sulphate.
25. $Hg Cl_2$ . . . . Mercuric Chloride.
26. $Ag NO_3$ . . . . Argentic Nitrate, (Amber.)
27. $Pb (C_2 H_3 O_2)_2$. Plumbic Acetate.
28. $Fe SO_4$ . . . . Ferrous Sulphate.
29. $Fe Cl_6$ . . . . . Ferric Chloride.
30. $C_2 H_6 O$ . . . . Alcohol.

No.
31. $N H_4 Cy S$ . . . Ammonic Sulphocyanide.
32. $Ba (HO)_2$ . . . Baric Hydrate.
33. $Ba CO_3$ . . . . Baric Carbonate.
34. $N H_4 C N S$ . . Ammonic Sulphocyanate.
35. $C_4 H_{10} O$ . . . . Ether.
36. $Cu SO_4$ . . . . Cupric Sulphate.
37. $Pt Cl_4$ . . . . . Platinic Chloride.
38, 39, 40. Blank.

The above 40 Bottles (3 Blanks) are sold in a set, and will be forwarded on the receipt of $5.83 *net.*

41. $H C_2 H_3 O_2$ . . Symbols only.
42. $N H_4 Cl$ . . . .   "   "
43. $(N H_4)_2 CO_3$ . .   "   "
44. $(N H_4)_2 C_2 O_4$.   "   "
45. $(N H_4)_2 S$ . . .   "   "
46. $Na_2 H PO_4$ . . .   "   "
47. $Ba Cl_2$ . . . . .   "   "
48. $Ba (NO_3)_2$ . . .   "   "
49. $Ca SO_4$ . . . .   "   "
50. $Mg SO_4$ . . . .   "   "
51. $Fe Cl_6$ . . . . .   "   "
52. $K_4 Fe Cy_6$ . . .   "   "
53. $K_3 Fe Cy_6$ . . .   "   "
54. $K_2 Cr_2 O_7$ . . .   "   "
55. $Pb (C_2 H_3 O_2)_2$.   "   "
56. No Symbols . . Uranic Acetate.
57. $Hg (NO_3)_2$ . . . Mercuric Nitrate.
58. No Symbols . . Fehling's Solution.
59. $Na_2 CO_3$ . . . . Sodic Carbonate.
60. $Na C_2 H_3 O_2$ . . Sodic Acetate.
61. $Na O H$ . . . . Sodic Hydrate.
62. No Symbols . . Baryta Mixture.
63. $H NO_2$ . . . . Acid Nitrous.
64. $H_3 PO_4$ . . . . Symbols only.

Net Price per Doz, $1.75. Per Gross, $18.50 *net.*

CHEMICAL REAGENT BOTTLES.

No.	Formula	Name
65.	$Na_2 H P O_4$	Sodic Phosphate.
66.	$C_2 H_4 O_2$	Acetic Acid.
67.	$H N O_3$	Nitric Acid.
68.	$Fe_2 Cl_6$	Ferric Chloride.
69.	$H_2 S C_4$	Sulphuric Acid.
70.	$Na_2 S O_4$	Sodic Sulphate.
71.	$(N H_4)_2 (C O_3)_3 L_2$	Ammonic Carbonate.
72.	H Cl	Hydrochloric Acid.
73.	$K_4 Fe_2 Cy_6$	Potassic Ferrocyanide.
75.	Na H O	Sodic Hydrate.
76.	I	Iodine.
77.	$N H_3$	Ammonia.
78.	$Pb 2 C_2 H_3 O_2 2 Pb O$	Basic Plumbic Acetate.
79.	No Symbols	Millon's Reagent.
80.	$C_2 H_2 O_4$	Hydric Oxalate.

Net Price per Dozen, $1.75. Per Gross, $18.50 Net.

6 OZ. REAGENT BOTTLES.
[Same lettering as Nos. 1–80.]
Net Price per Dozen, $2.00. Per Gross, $21.00 Net.

4 OZ. SALT MOUTHS.

No.   SYMBOLS ONLY.
- 301. $Na_2 CO_3$.
- 302. $K N O_3$.
- 303. K C N.
- 304. $Na_2 B_4 O_7$.
- 305. $Fe SO_4$.
- 306. $Na (N H_4) H P O_4 + 4 H_2 O$.
- 307. Blank.
- 308. $Na NO_3$.

Net Price per Dozen, $1.93. Per Gross, $20.50 Net.

HALF PINT REAGENT BOTTLES, 1-4 LITER.

No.	Formula	Name
101.	$H_2 SO_4$	Sulphuric Acid, (Concent.)
102.	$H_2 SO_4 + Aq$	Sulphuric Acid, (Dilute.)
103.	$H N O_3 + Aq$	Nitric Acid, (Concent.)
104.	$H N O_3 + Aq$	Nitric Acid, (Dilute.)
105.	$H Cl + Aq$	Hydrochloric Acid, (Conc't.)
106.	$H Cl + Aq$	Hydrochloric Acid, (Dilute.)
107.	$H_2 S$	Hydric Sulphide.
108.	$H_4 N H O$	Ammonic Hydrate.
109.	$H_4 N Cl + Aq$	Ammonic Chloride.
110.	$(H_4 N)_2 CO_3 + Aq$	Ammonic Carbonate.
111.	$Na O H + Aq$	Sodic Hydrate.
112.	$Na_2 CO_3$	Sodic Carbonate.
113.	$H_4 N S H + Aq$	Ammonic Sulphydrate.
114.	$Ba Cl_2 + Aq$	Baric Chloride.
115.	$Ca Cl_2 + Aq$	Calcic Chloride.
116, 117, 118.	Blank.	
119.	$H_2 SO_4$	Hydric Sulphate.
120.	H Cl	Hydric Chloride.
121.	$H N O_3$	Hydric Nitrate.
122.	$(N H_4)_2 S$	Ammonic Sulphide, (Amber.)
123.	$Ba CO_3$	Baric Carbonate.
124.	$Ba O H_2 O$	Baric Hydrate.
125.	$C_3 H_8 O_3$	Glycerine.
126.	$C_2 H_6 O$	Alcohol.
127.	$C_2 H_4 O_2$	Hydric Acetate.
128.	$K_4 Cfy$	Potassic Ferrocyanide.
129.	$Na H_2 P O_4$	Sodic Phosphate.
130.	$(N H_4)_2 C_2 C_4$	Ammonic Oxalate.
131.	$H C_2 H_3 O_2$	Acetic Acid.
132.	$C_2 H_{10} O$	Ether.
133.	Con. $H_2 SO_4$	Symbols only.
134.	Con. $H N O_3$	" "
135.	Con. H Cl	" "
136.	Dil. $H_2 SO_4$	" "
137.	Dil. $H N O_3$	" "
138.	Dil. H Cl	Symbols only.
139.	$N H_4 H O$	" "
140.	Na H O	" "
141.	$Na_2 CO_3$	" "
142.	$K_3 Cfy$	Potassic Ferricyanide.
143.	K I	Potassic Iodide.
144.	$K_2 Cr_2 O_7$	Potassic Acid Chromate.
145.	$Ag NO_3$	Argentic Nitrate, (Amber.)
146.	$Fe Cl_6$	Ferric Chloride.

Net Price per Dozen, $2.25. Per Gross, $23.00 Net.

PINT REAGENT BOTTLES, 1-2 LITER.

No.	Formula	Name
201.	$H_2 S O_4 + Aq$	Sulphuric Acid, (Dilute.)
202.	$H N O_3 + Aq$	Nitric Acid, (Dilute.)
203.	$H Cl + Aq$	Hydrochloric Acid, (Dilute.)
204.	$H_4 N H O$	Ammonic Hydrate.
205.	$H_4 N Cl + Aq$	Ammonic Chloride.
206.	$(H_4 N)_2 CO_3 + Aq$	Ammonic Carbonate.
207.	No Symbols	Dil. Nitro-Hydr. Acid.
208.	No Symbols	Liquor Potassæ.
209.	No Symbols	Tinct. Ferri Perchlor.
210.	$H_2 S$	Hydric Sulphide.
211, 212.	Blank	
213.	$H_3 PO_4 + Aq$	Phosphoric Acid, (Dil.)
214.	$(N H_4)_2 S$	Ammonic Sulphide.
215.	$H_2 S O_4 + Aq$	Sulphuric Acid.
216.	$H N O_3 + Aq$	Nitric Acid.
217.	$H Cl + Aq$	Hydrochloric Acid.
251.	$K O H + Aq$	Symbols only.
252.	$H_2 SO_4 + Aq$ Dil	" "
253.	$H Cl + Aq$ Dil	" "
254.	$H NO_3 + Aq$ Dil	" "
255.	$(N H_4) O H + Aq$	" "
256.	$(N H_4)_2 CO_3 + Aq$	" "
257.	$(N H_4) Cl + Aq$	" "
258.	$(N H_4) S H + Aq$	" "
259.	$Ba Cl_2 + Aq$	" "
260.	$Ca Cl_2 + Aq$	" "
261.	$H_2 SO_4$	" "
262.	$H Cl + Aq$ Conc.	" "
263.	$H NO_3 + Aq$ Conc	" "
264.	$Pb (C_2 H_3 O_2)_2 + Aq$	" "
265.	$Ca SO_4 + Aq$	" "
266.	$H (C_2 H_3 O_2) + Aq$	" "
267.	$H Na_2 P O_4 + Aq$	" "
268.	$Ag N O_3 + Aq$	" "
269.	$(N H_4)_2 C_2 O_4$	Ammonic Oxalate.
270.	$Ba CO_3$	Baric Carbonate.
271.	$Na_2 CO_3$	Sodic Carbonate.
272.	Na O H	Sodic Hydrate.

Net Price per Dozen, $3.25. Per Gross, $33.00 Net.

1 OZ. REAGENTS.

- 325. $Ag N O_3$ . . . . Symbols only.
- 326. $Co (N O_3)_2$ . . . " "
- 327. $Pt Cl_4$ . . . . . " "
- 328. $Hg Cl_2$ . . . . . " "

Net Price per Dozen, $1.25. Per Gross, $12.00 Net.

1 OZ. SALT MOUTH REAGENTS.

- 350. $Na_2 C O_3$ . . . . Symbols only.
- 351. $Na_2 B_4 O_7$ . . . " "
- 352. $H_2 C_4 H_4 O_6$ . . " "
- 353. $Na C_2 H_3 O_2$ . . " "
- 354. $K N O_3$ . . . . " "
- 355. Fe S . . . . . " "

Net Price per Dozen, $1.35. Per Gross, $13.00 Net.

For the unlettered Tincture and Salt-Mouth Bottles, Stoppered and Corks, see pages 14, 26.

CHEMICAL WARE.

No. 2000. CHEMICAL FLASKS.

With or without Lips.

FLAT BOTTOMS.

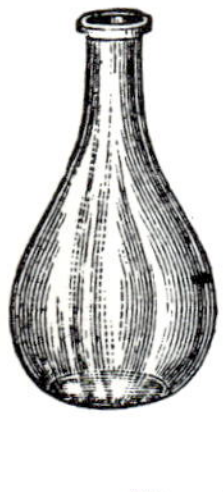

Content	Per dozen.
1 ounce	$2 00
2 ounce	2 00
4 ounce	2 50
6 ounce	2 90
½ Pint	3 25
Pint	4 50
Quart	5 50
½ Gallon	9 00
1 Gallon	16 00

No. 2010. CHEMICAL FLASKS.

ROUND BOTTOM.

Content	Per dozen.
1 ounce	$2 00
2 ounce	2 00
4 ounce	2 50
6 ounce	2 90
½ Pint	3 25
Pint	4 50
Quart	5 50
½ Gallon	9 00
1 Gallon	16 00

No. 2020. ASSAY FLASKS.

(ERLENMEYER.)

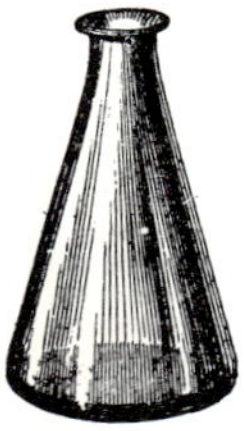

Content	Per dozen.
1 ounce	$2 00
2 ounce	2 00
4 ounce	2 50
½ Pint	3 25
Pint	4 50
Quart	5 50
½ Gallon	9 00

NO. 2030. FLASKS FOR MEASURING.

	Per Dozen.		GRADUATED.	
	For Corks.	Stoppered.	For Corks.	Stop'd.
¼ Liter	$4 50	$7 50	$8 00	$11 00
½ Liter	5 50	8 50	12 00	15 00
1 Liter	9 00	12 00	21 00	24 00
2 Liter	12 00	15 00	27 00	30 00

Side Neck Flasks 50% advance on above prices. Double marks on Graduated Flasks 50% advance.

No. 2050. BEAKER GLASSES.

TALL.

Content.	Size.	Per dozen.
1 ounce	2⅛x1½ in.	$1 10
2 ounce	2⅜x1⅝ in.	1 10

No. 2050. TALL BEAKER GLASSES. (Cont'd.)

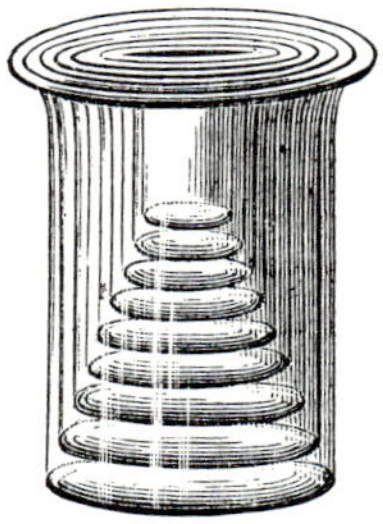

Content.	Size	Per dozen.
3 oz.	2¾x1¾	$1 65
4 oz.	3 x1⅞	2 20
6 oz.	3¼x2¼	2 75
8 oz.	3¾x2⅜	3 60
10 oz.	4¼x2½	3 80
12 oz.	4½x2¾	4 00
16 oz.	5 x3	4 50
24 oz.	5½x3¼	6 30
32 oz.	6¼x3½	7 20
40 oz.	7⅛x3¾	7 70
48 ounce	7¾x4	8 10
56 ounce	8½x4⅛	8 70
64 ounce	9¼x4½	9 00

With LIPS, ten per cent. extra.

No. 2060. BEAKER GLASSES.

WIDE.

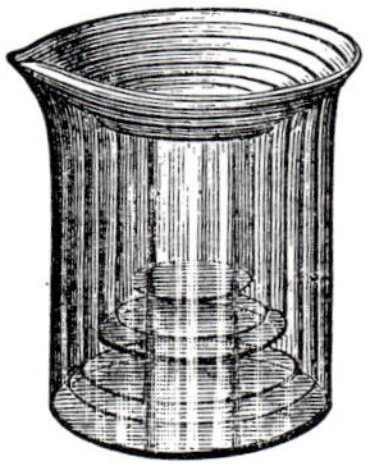

Content.	Size.	Per dozen.
1 oz.	2 x1⅜	$1 10
2 oz.	2¼x1⅝	1 10
3 oz.	2½x1⅞	1 65
4 oz.	2¾x2	2 20
6 oz.	3 x2¼	2 75
8 oz.	3½x2½	3 60
10 oz.	3¾x2¾	3 80
12 oz.	4 x3	4 00
16 oz.	4¼x3¼	4 50
24 ounce	5 x3⅝	6 30
32 ounce	6 x4	7 20
48 ounce	6¾x4¼	8 10
64 ounce	7½x4¾	9 00

With LIPS ten per cent. extra.

NESTED BEAKER GLASSES.

Each Nest in a paste-board box. Beakers nested in any assortment desired at same prices as separate.

			Each Nest.
No. 2070.	**Nest of 5.**	1, 2, 3, 4 and 6 oz.	$ 74
No. 2071.	" **6.**	1, 2, 3, 4, 6 and 8 oz.	1 04
No. 2072.	" **9.**	1, 2, 3, 4, 6, 8, 10, 12 and 16 oz	2 06
No. 2073.	" **11.**	1, 2, 3, 4, 6, 8, (10, 12, 16, 24 and 32 oz.)	3 19
No. 2074.	" **13.**	1, 2, 3, 4, 6, 8, 10, 12, 16, 24, 32, 40, 48 oz.	4 50
No. 2075.	" **15.**	1, 2, 3, 4, 6, 8, 10, 12, 16, 24, 32, 40, 48, 56 and 64 oz.	5 98

CHEMICAL WARE.

RETORTS.

	No. 2100. Plain.	No. 2110. Tubulated.
	Plain.	Tubulated.
	Per Doz.	
1/8 Pint	$3 50	$4 00
1/4 Pint	3 80	5 50
1/2 Pint	5 00	7 00
Pint	9 00	10 00
Quart	11 00	12 00
1/2 Gallon	16 00	18 00
Gallon	20 00	24 00
2 Gallon	40 00	48 00
3 Gallon	52 00	70 00
4 Gallon	60 00	90 00
5 Gallon	80 00	130 00

No. 2120. Stoppered.

Per Doz.
1/8 Pint	6 80
1/4 Pint	7 50
1/2 Pint	9 00
Pint	11 00
Quart	13 50
1/2 Gallon	20 00
Gallon	26 00
2 Gallon	50 00
3 Gallon	76 00
4 Gallon	100 00
5 Gallon	150 00

RECEIVERS.

	No. 2125. Plain.	No. 2128. Tubulated.
	Plain.	Tubulated.
	Per Doz.	
1/4 Pint	3 80	5 50
1/2 Pint	5 00	7 00
Pint	9 00	10 00
Quart	11 00	12 00
1/2 Gallon	16 00	18 00
Gallon	20 00	24 00
2 Gallon	40 00	48 00

No. 2130. Stoppered.

Per Doz.
1/4 Pint	7 50
1/2 Pint	9 00
Pint	11 00
Quart	13 50
1/2 Gallon	20 00
Gallon	26 00

The above Retorts and Receivers can be made of extra weight for distilling mercury, &c.

IRON SUPPORTS, 3 Rings, $3 50 each.

No. 2145. OXYGEN GLOBES.

10 inch	$2.00 each.
12 inch	2.50 each.
15 inch	5.00 each.

No. 2150. TEST TUBES.

Per gross.
3 inch	$3 50
4 inch	3 75
5 inch	4 50
6 inch	5 25
7 inch	6 75
8 inch	9 00
9 inch	13 59
10 inch	18 00
11 inch	21 00
12 inch	24 00

NESSLER COMPARISON TUBES.

Per Dozen.
Flat on bottom	6 00

Test Tubes Nested.

Per Doz. Nests.
2160.	4 to 6 inch	1 15
2161.	3 to 6 inch	1 40
2162.	3 to 7 inch	2 00
2163.	3 to 9 inch	3 85

No. 2165. TEST TUBES ON FOOT.

Per doz.
3 inch	1 00
4 inch	1 10
5 inch	1 50
6 inch	1 80
7 inch	2 00
8 inch	2 25
9 inch	2 75
10 inch	3 50
11 inch	4 50
12 inch	5 50

No. 2170. IGNITION TUBES.

Per doz.
3 inch	$ 60
4 inch	70
5 inch	80
6 inch	90
7 inch	1 00
8 inch	1 50
9 inch	2 25
10 inch	3 00
11 inch	3 50
12 inch	4 00

Nested to order at same prices as separate.

No. 2175. SIDE NECK TEST TUBES.

After Prof. J. H. Appleton's Design.

	Per doz.
5 inch	80
6 inch	90
7 inch	1 00
8 inch	1 50
9 inch	2 25

No. 2177. SIDE NECK IGNITION TUBES.

	Per Doz.
5 inch	1 20
6 inch	1 35
7 inch	1 50
8 inch	2 25
9 inch	3 40

No. 2180. FUNNELS.

By an arrangement of our own device, we are able to make Chemical Funnels of the correct angle and best shape for preserving the filter paper.

PLAIN OR FLUTED.   ANGLE OF 60°.

		Per doz.
1 ounce,	2¼ inch	1 35
2 ounce,	2¾ inch	1 50
¼ Pint,	3½ inch	2 00
½ Pint,	4½ inch	2 25
Pint,	5½ inch	3 00
Quart,	7 inch	3 40
½ Gallon,	9 inch	4 50
1 Gallon,	10½ inch	7 00
2 Gallon,	12 inch	11 00

No. 2190. SEPARATING STOPPERED FUNNELS.

		Each
½ Pint,	4 inch	$3 75
Pint,	5½ inch	4 50
Quart,	7 inch	5 25
½ Gallon,	9 inch	6 00
Gallon,	10½ inch	7 00

No. 2195. GAS BOTTLES.

	Per doz.
½ Pint	$4 00
Pint	5 00
Quart	7 00
½ Gallon	11 00
Gallon	18 00

MISCELLANEOUS LAMP WORK.

2200.
2201.

	Per Doz.
2200. Tube Funnel	$3 20
2201. Tube Funnel, Thistle Mouth	3 20

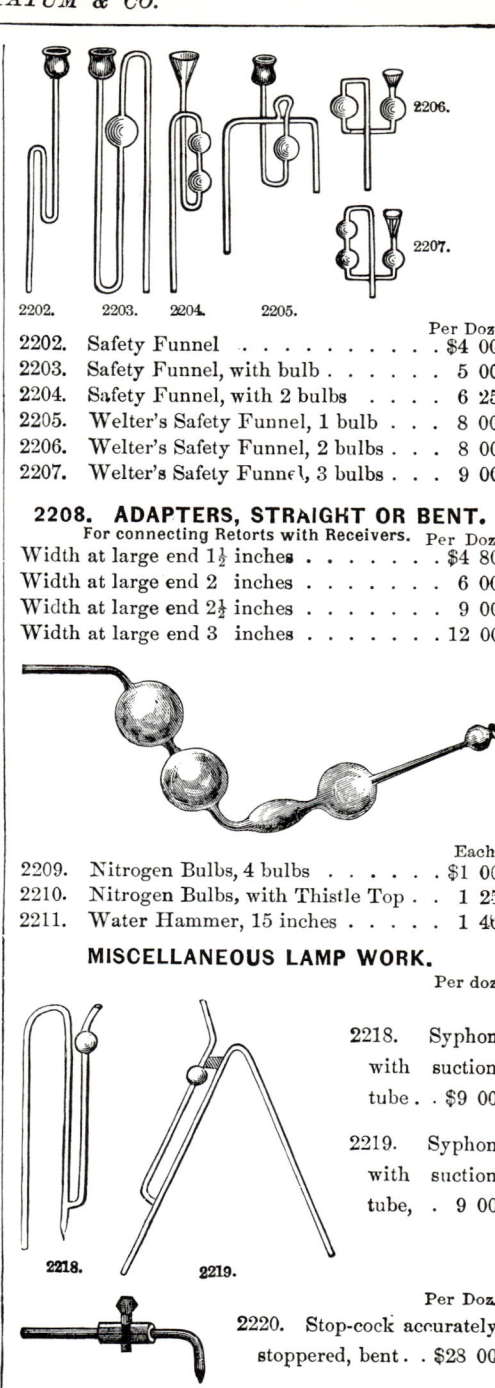

2202. 2203. 2204. 2205. 2206. 2207.

	Per Doz.
2202. Safety Funnel	$4 00
2203. Safety Funnel, with bulb	5 00
2204. Safety Funnel, with 2 bulbs	6 25
2205. Welter's Safety Funnel, 1 bulb	8 00
2206. Welter's Safety Funnel, 2 bulbs	8 00
2207. Welter's Safety Funnel, 3 bulbs	9 00

2208. ADAPTERS, STRAIGHT OR BENT.

For connecting Retorts with Receivers.

	Per Doz.
Width at large end 1½ inches	$4 80
Width at large end 2 inches	6 00
Width at large end 2½ inches	9 00
Width at large end 3 inches	12 00

	Each.
2209. Nitrogen Bulbs, 4 bulbs	$1 00
2210. Nitrogen Bulbs, with Thistle Top	1 25
2211. Water Hammer, 15 inches	1 40

MISCELLANEOUS LAMP WORK.

	Per doz
2218. Syphon with suction tube	$9 00
2219. Syphon with suction tube,	9 00

2218. 2219.

	Per Doz.
2220. Stop-cock accurately stoppered, bent	$28 00
2221. Stop-cock accurately stoppered, straight	28 00

CHEMICAL WARE.

	Per doz.
2222. Liebig's Potash bulb	13 00
2223. Mitcherlich Potash bulb	13 00

No. 2224. U TUBES.

	Per doz.
3 inch	$3 00
4 inch	3 60
5 inch	4 20
6 inch	4 80
7 inch	6 40
8 inch	8 00
9 inch	9 60
12 inch	18 00

Side Neck U Tubes, 50 per cent advance over plain.

	Per Doz.
2225. Glass Pipette	$4 00
2226. Glass Pipette	4 00
2227. Glass Pipette	4 00

VOLUME PIPETTES TO DELIVER
2225, 2226 & 2227. Each.

1 Cubic centimetre	.20
2 Cubic "	.25
5 Cubic "	.30
10 Cubic "	.40
15 Cubic "	.40
20 Cubic "	.50
25 Cubic "	.60
50 Cubic "	.65
100 Cubic "	.85

2233. Tube Connection	$4 50
2234. Tube Connection	3 60

	Per doz.
2228. Chloride of Calcium tube	$3 00
2229. Chloride of Calcium tube	3 00
2230. Chloride of Calcium tube	3 00
2231. Dropping glass,	5 00
2232. Dropping glass, stoppered	6 50
2235. T Tube	4 80
2240. Y Tube	4 80

No 2265. GLASS DISHES.

	Each.
3 inch diameter	50
6 inch diameter	1 00
9 inch diameter	2 00
2270. Glass Spoons	65

No. 2275. GROUND GLASS PLATES.

	Each.
3 inches square	20
4 inches square	30
5 inches square	40
6 inches square	50

No. 2280. WEIGHING BOTTLE.
VERY LIGHT.

	Each.
1 oz.	$ 40
2 oz.	50
4 oz.	60
16 oz. Straight Sides	2 00

GLASS TUBING—Light and Heavy.

2285. Per lb 60

Special prices in large quantities.

GLASS RODS.

2287. Per lb 50

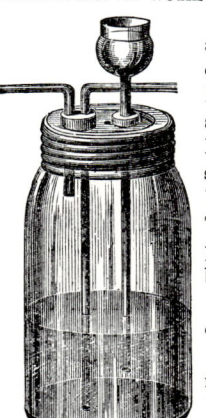

		Each.
2290. Kipp's Gas Generator, . . .		10 50

		Per Doz.
2295. Bunsen's Carbonic Acid Apparatus, . . .		36 00
2294. Geissler's Carbonic Acid Apparatus, . . .		36 00

No. 2300. GLASS MORTARS AND PESTLES.

		Per Doz.
1 oz. . .	2¼ in. wide . .	4 80
2 oz. . .	2¾ in. wide . .	4 80
3 oz. . .	3 in. wide . .	6 00
4 oz. . .	3¾ in. wide . .	6 00
8 oz. . .	4½ in. wide . .	9 60
12 oz. . .	5 in. wide	11 00
Pint . .	5½ in. wide	12 00
Quart . .	7 in. wide	18 00
3 Pint . .	8 in. wide	24 00

Also WEDGWOOD Mortars. See page 65.

No. 2320. WOULFF BOTTLES.

TWO OR THREE NECKS.

	Each.
¼ Pint	80
½ Pint	1 00
Pint	1 30
Quart	1 80
½ Gallon	2 50
Gallon	4 50

No. 2326. WITH TUBULATURE NEAR BOTTOM.

	Each.
¼ Pint	1 60
½ Pint	1 80
Pint	2 20
Quart	3 10
½ Gallon	4 50
Gallon	7 10

2340. MILLVILLE CHEMICAL JAR.

A Substitute for Woulff Bottles, Chemical Flasks, &c.

We call attention to this Jar as more convenient and less expensive than the Woulff Bottle, now in use. It consists of a Glass Jar with a Perforated Glass Lid, closed securely by means of a Metal Ring and Rubber Packing. Through the Perforations pass the Glass Tubes, secured by Rubber Corks. See Cut.

1. It is easily charged emptied and cleansed.
2. It is made of glass carefully annealed for use in the Water Bath.
3. The fittings are interchangeable with all sizes.
4. A solid lid also accompanies each Jar, which can be used for preserving deliquescent salts.
5. The Rubber Ring and Corks are of superior quality and will last for years. They should be made wet before using.

Price, with Solid and Perforated Lids, Rubber Corks, and Tubing, Ready for use.

	Each.
½ Pints	80
Pints	1 00
Quarts	1 50
½ Gallon	2 00
1 Gallon	2 75

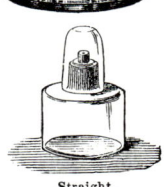

No. 2346. ACID DROP OR COIN TEST BOTTLES.

	Per Dozen.	With Glass Caps.
1 oz.	6 00 . . .	10 00
2 oz.	7 25 . . .	11 25

2350. SPIRIT LAMPS.

Straight.   Globe.

	Per Doz.
1½ oz. TAPER—Fitted	5 00
3 oz. TAPER—Fitted	7 00
3 oz. STRAIGHT—Fitted	6 50
4 oz. GLOBE—Fitted	8 00

No. 2353. PROOF GLASSES.

PROOF GLASSES 3 50

GLASS TUBING.

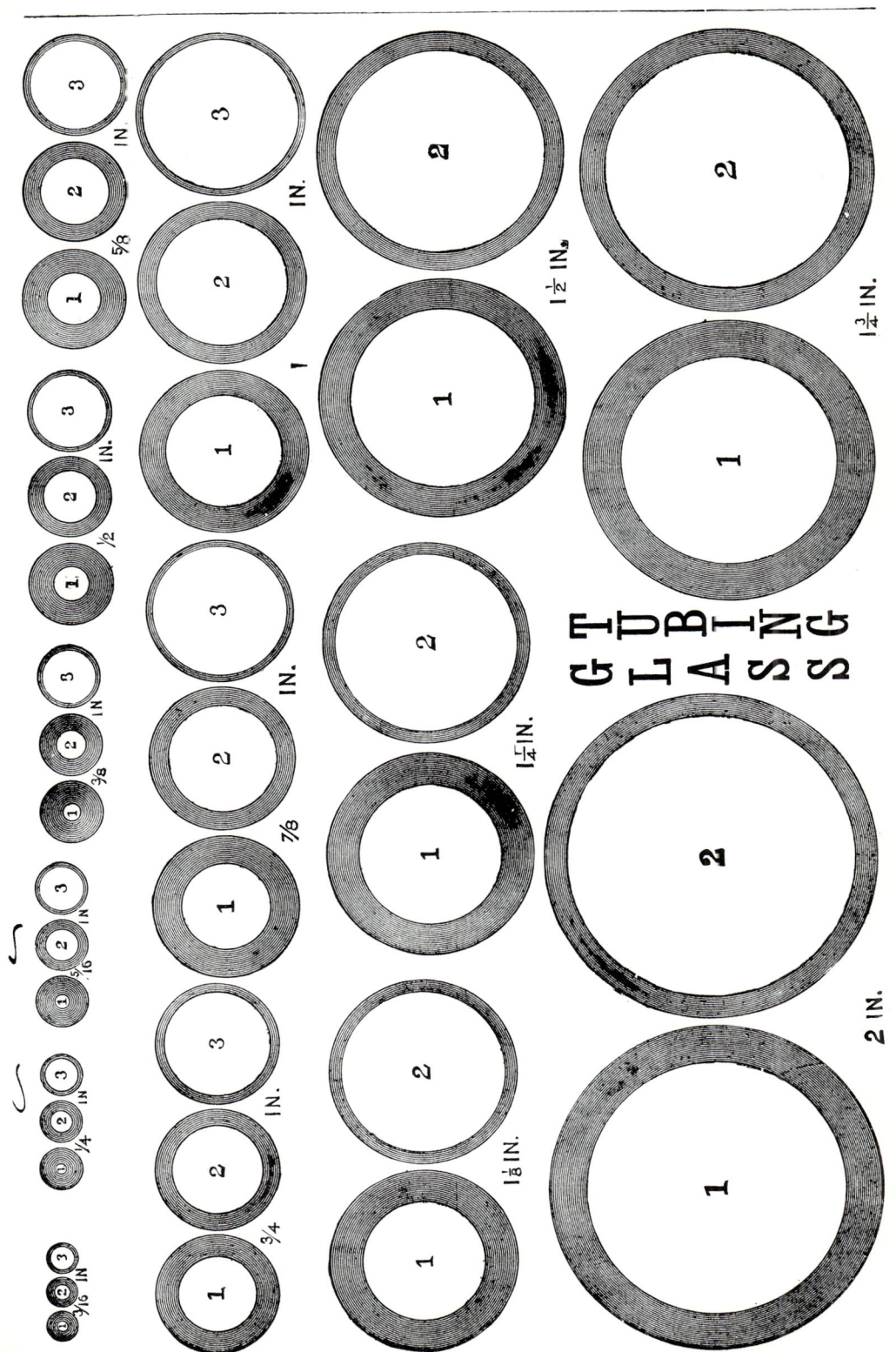

No. 2355. CHLORIDE CALCIUM JARS.

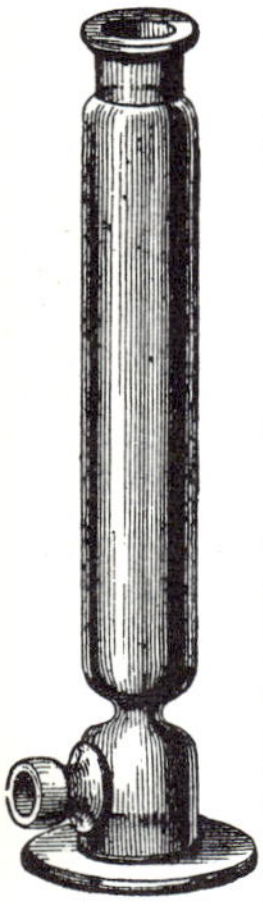

	Each.
12 x 2 inch	$1 75
17 x 2½ inch	2 50
21 x 3 inch	4 00

No. 2360. PERCOLATORS.

(Stoppered $2.25 net, extra for each Percolator.)

Graduated, see page 64.

	Per Doz.
½ Pint	4 00
Pint	6 00
Quart	8 00
½ Gallon	12 00
Gallon	16 00
1½ Gallon	22 00
2 Gallon	28 00
3 Gallon	54 00

With supporting RING on side, if so ordered.
Percolator Weights inches diameter.

No. 2370. PRECIPITATING JARS.

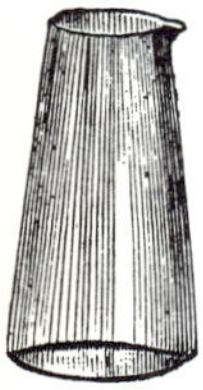

	Per Doz.
¼ Pint	3 00
½ Pint	3 75
Pint	5 00
Quart	7 25
½ Gallon	12 50
Gallon	17 00
1½ Gallon	25 00
2 Gallon	31 00
3 Gallon	56 00

No. 2380. EVAPORATING DISHES—GLASS.

PLAIN.

	Per Doz.
2 inches diameter	2 60
3 inches diameter	3 30
4 inches diameter	4 00
5 inches diameter	4 80
6 inches diameter	5 30

NESTS.

	Each Nest.
2385. Nest of 2, 3, 4 inch	85
2386. Nest of 4, 5, 6 inch	1 20
2387. Nest of 2, 3, 4, 5, 6 inch	1 70

No. 2390. WITH LIPS.

	Per Doz.
2 inches diameter	3 20
3 inches diameter	4 10
4 inches diameter	5 00
5 inches diameter	6 00
6 inches diameter	6 60

NESTS.

	Each Nest.
2395. Nest of 2, 3, 4 inch	1 00
2396. Nest of 4, 5, 6 inch	1 50
2397. Nest of 2, 3, 4, 5, 6 inch	2 10

No. 2398. WATCH GLASSES.

	Per Doz.
2 inch	$2 60
3 inch	3 30
4 inch	4 00
5 inch	4 80
6 inch	5 30

Nested at same price as single.

No. 2400. BOTTLES WITH TUBULATURE.

NOT STOPPERED.

	Per Doz.
½ Pint	6 00
Pint	8 20
1½ Pint	10 00
Quart	12 00
3 Pint	14 00
½ Gallon	16 00
Gallon	24 00
2 Gallon	60 00

No. 2410. BOTTLES WITH TUBULATURE.

STOPPERED.

	Per Doz.
½ Pint	7 75
Pint	10 50
1½ Pint	12 50
Quart	14 50
3 Pint	18 00
½ Gallon	20 00
1 Gallon	30 00
2 Gallon	75 00

No. 2420. STOPPERED.

With Tubulature and Glass Tap Ground into the Tubulature.

	Each.
½ Pint	4 00
Pint	4 25
1½ Pint	5 00
Quart	5 50
3 Pint	6 00
½ Gallon	6 50
1 Gallon	10 00
2 Gallon	25 00

No. 2430. INVERTED SHOW BOTTLES.

STRAIGHT.

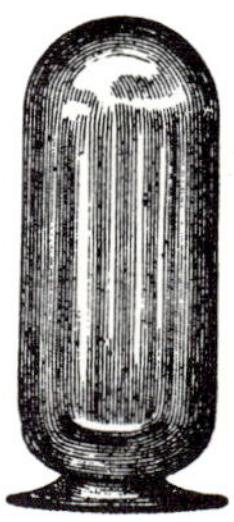

	Each.
½ Pint, 5 x 2 in.	40
Pint, 7½ x 2¾ in.	50
Quart, 9 x 3¼ in.	75
½ Gallon, 11 x 4½ in.	1 20
Gallon, 14 x 5¾ in.	1 90
2 Gallon, 16 x 6¾ in.	4 00
3 Gallon, 19 x 8 in.	6 00
½ Bushel, 27 x 10 in.	11 00
32 x 12½ in.	14 00

CHEMICAL WARE.

No. 2440. INVERTED SHOW BOTTLES.
PEAR SHAPE.

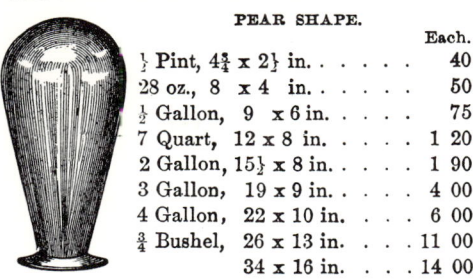

	Each.
½ Pint, 4¾ x 2½ in.	40
28 oz., 8 x 4 in.	50
½ Gallon, 9 x 6 in.	75
7 Quart, 12 x 8 in.	1 20
2 Gallon, 15½ x 8 in.	1 90
3 Gallon, 19 x 9 in.	4 00
4 Gallon, 22 x 10 in.	6 00
¾ Bushel, 26 x 13 in.	11 00
34 x 16 in.	14 00

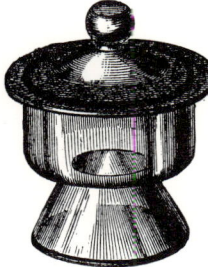

No. 2450. DESICCATING JAR.
WITH GROUND LID.

	Dozen.
4 inches diameter	18 00

No. 2460. SPECIMEN BOTTLES.
STOPPERED.

	Per Doz.
1 oz.	2 70
2 oz.	3 00
4 oz.	4 00

No. 2500. BELL GLASSES.
Special Dimensions Made to Order.
SHORT-KNOB.

	Each.
Pint	75
Quart	1 00
½ Gallon	1 50
Gallon	2 00
2 Gallon	3 00
3 Gallon	5 00
5 Gallon	10 00

Bell Glasses, Flat or Tall, not ground for Covers, one-fifth less in price.

No. 2510. TALL-KNOB.

	Each.
Pint	75
Quart	1 00
½ Gallon	1 50
Gallon	2 00
2 Gallon	3 00
3 Gallon	5 00
5 Gallon	10 00

No. 2520. OPEN TOP.

	Each.
Pint	80
Quart	1 10
½ Gallon	1 60
Gallon	2 20
2 Gallon	3 80
3 Gallon	5 50
5 Gallon	11 00

No. 2530. NARROW MOUTH FOR CAPS.

	Each.
Pint	80
Quart	1 10
½ Gallon	1 60
Gallon	2 20

TUBULATED NEAR THE BOTTOM DOUBLE PRICE.

No. 2550. SHORT BELL GLASSES.
NOT GROUND.

	Each.
4 inch	50
6 inch	75
8 inch	1 30
10 inch	1 60
12 inch	1 90

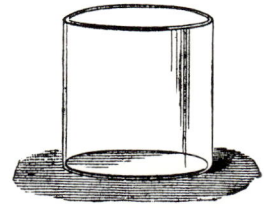

No. 2580. GLASS BATTERY JARS.

Wide.		High.		Each.
4	x	4	inches outside	30
4	x	5	inches outside	45
4½	x	5½	inches outside	54
4½	x	6	inches outside	75
5½	x	8	inches outside	90
7	x	8	inches outside	1 20
6	x	9	inches outside	1 30
8	x	12	inches outside	1 80
9	x	12½	inches outside	3 00
9	x	15	inches outside	3 20

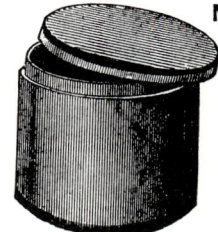

No. 2590. GLASS BOXES.
WITH GLASS LIDS.

	Per Doz.
½ oz.	1 40
1 oz.	1 50
2 oz.	1 80
4 oz.	2 10
8 oz.	2 60
16 oz.	3 30

See 4 oz. Ground Top Box, No. 634, Page 63.

2600. MUSEUM JARS.

FOR PRESERVING SPECIMENS.

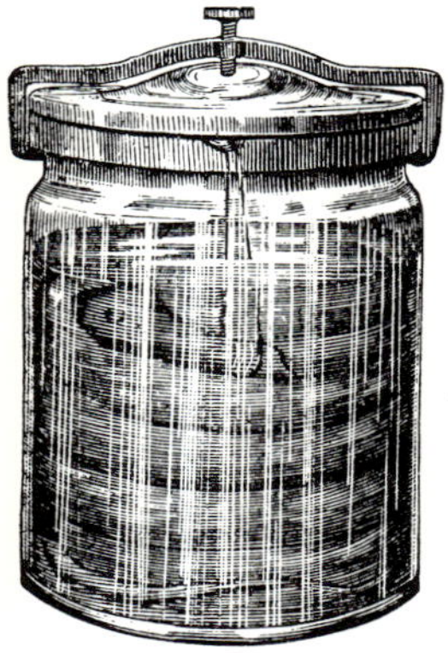

Several scientific gentlemen having brought to our notice the absence in the market of a complete Specimen Preserving Jar, at their suggestion we have prepared an article which meets their entire approval.

The contents are enclosed entirely in glass, with a thin rubber medium under the lid to make the jar air-tight. This lid is securely fastened down with an outer metallic clamp. On the inner surface of the Glass Lid is attached a glass ring, for the convenient securing of specimens.

The good points of these Jars are their *simplicity*, their *wide mouths*, *glass* instead of metallic lids, *easiness of access* to the specimens, and *security* against the evaporation of the contents. They are in use widely in public Museums.

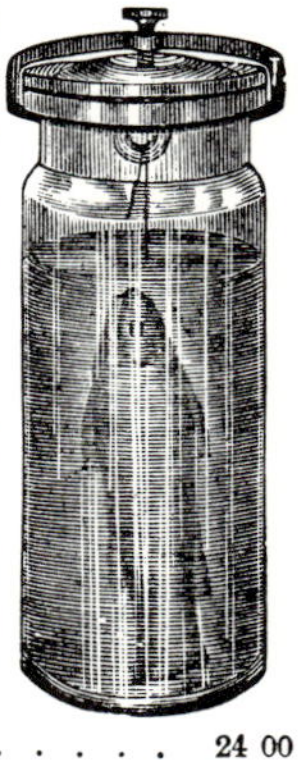

It will be noticed below that we make them of thirteen different dimensions, with four different diameters, having capacities ranging from ½ Pint to five Gallons.

SIZES. Wide. High.	CAPACITIES.	PRICE. Per Doz.
3 in. by 4 in.,	½ Pint,	$6 00
3 in. by 7 in.,	Pint,	8 00
3 in. by 10 in.,	Quart,	9 00
4½ in. by 6 in.,	Quart,	9 00
4½ in. by 8½ in.,	3 Pint,	11 00
4½ in. by 11½ in.,	½ Gall.	12 00
6 in. by 8 in.,	1 Gall.	20 00
6 in. by 12 in.,	1½ Gall.	24 00
6 in. by 15 in.,	1¾ Gall.	26 00
6 in. by 18 in.,	2 Gall.	28 00
9 in. by 12 in.,	2½ Gall.	40 00
9 in. by 18 in.,	3½ Gall.	60 00
9 in. by 23 in.,	5 Gall.	120 00

Special lengths of the above diameters made to order. Content is approximate only.

Without LIDS or FITTINGS at two-thirds of the above prices.

The above Jars, with holes drilled through the Lid, are well suited for Gas Generators and other Chemical purposes:

	Each.
Price with 1 hole	$1 00 extra.
Price with 2 holes	2 00 extra.
Price with 3 holes	2 50 extra.

No. 2700. HYDROMETER JARS.

On Foot. Lip or Plain.

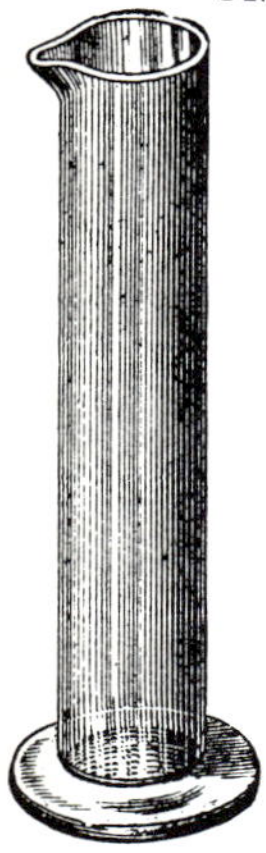

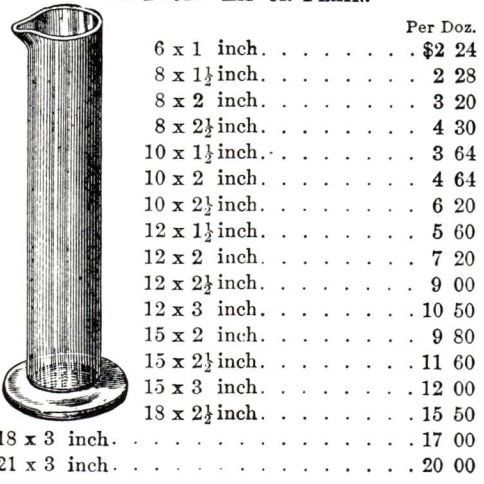

	Per Doz.
6 x 1 inch	$2 24
8 x 1½ inch	2 28
8 x 2 inch	3 20
8 x 2½ inch	4 30
10 x 1½ inch	3 64
10 x 2 inch	4 64
10 x 2½ inch	6 20
12 x 1½ inch	5 60
12 x 2 inch	7 20
12 x 2½ inch	9 00
12 x 3 inch	10 50
15 x 2 inch	9 80
15 x 2½ inch	11 60
15 x 3 inch	12 00
18 x 2½ inch	15 50
18 x 3 inch	17 00
21 x 3 inch	20 00

Graduated, see p. 64. Same with Rim 10 per cent. add'l.

No. 2750. INSECT BOTTLES.

FOR CORKS.—EXTRA WIDTH OF MOUTH.

For Smaller Specimen Bottles we offer the following, which are made with **wide mouths**, and are furnished either for Corks or with Ground Glass Stoppers, at the prices noted below:

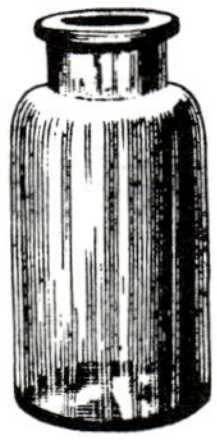

	Per Dozen. For Corks.	Glass Stoppers.
1¾ oz.	$ 80	$1 30
3 oz.	1 00	1 50
4 oz.	1 25	1 75
6 oz.	1 50	1 90

No. 2770. ANATOMICAL JARS.

	Per Doz.
Pint	5 00
Quart	7 25
½ Gallon	12 50
Gallon	17 00
1½ Gallon	25 00
2 Gallon	31 50

For Graduates, see page 61. For Tube Vials, see page 30.
For Corks, see page 66.

CATALOGUE
OF
GREEN GLASSWARE.

We call attention to our large assortment and heavy stock of Green Glass constantly on hand in New York and Philadelphia, as well as to its light color, secure packing and careful finish. An experience of over forty years in the business gives us confidence in soliciting orders.

We ask from those not acquainted with the reputation of our Green Glass a trial of a small lot, with a careful examination of the following points:

The great regularity of the mouths, allowing the use of the same size of cork.
The regularity of finish of the Lips or Rings.
The even distribution of the glass.
The careful annealing.
The small breakage.
The light color.
The smooth surface.
The modern style of our Drug Ware moulds.

Most of the Moulds in the list of Flint Glass can also be used in Green.

NO CHARGE FOR ORIGINAL PACKAGES.

A LIBERAL DISCOUNT TO THE TRADE.

Boxes containing a line of labeled samples of Green and Flint Glass will be sent to customers, upon application, at a nominal price.

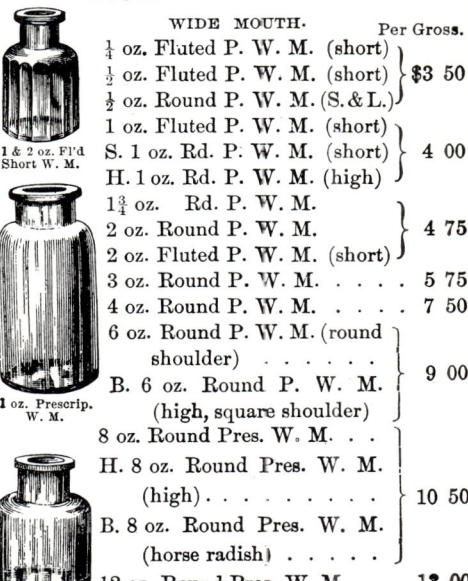

ROUND PRESCRIPTIONS.
FLUTED PRESCRIPTIONS, LONG and SHORT.
COMMON VIALS.

For Plates for Lettering various Styles of Bottles, see p. 9.

NARROW MOUTH.

	Per Gross.
Assorted in 1, 2, 3 & 5 gross boxes	$6 00
½ oz.	3 25
1 oz.	3 75
2 oz.	4 50
3 oz.	5 50
4 oz.	6 75
6 oz.	8 25
8 oz.	9 75
12 oz.	12 25
16 oz.	15 25
32 oz.	24 50
1¾ oz. F. P. L. S. 2 oz. F. P. L.	4 50
24 oz. F. P. L.	19 50
½, 1, 2 and 3 drachm Vials	3 75

ROUND PRESCRIPTIONS.

WIDE MOUTH.

	Per Gross.
¼ oz. Fluted P. W. M. (short)	
½ oz. Fluted P. W. M. (short)	$3 50
½ oz. Round P. W. M. (S. & L.)	
1 oz. Fluted P. W. M. (short)	
S. 1 oz. Rd. P. W. M. (short)	4 00
H. 1 oz. Rd. P. W. M. (high)	
1¾ oz. Rd. P. W. M.	
2 oz. Round P. W. M.	4 75
2 oz. Fluted P. W. M. (short)	
3 oz. Round P. W. M.	5 75
4 oz. Round P. W. M.	7 50
6 oz. Round P. W. M. (round shoulder)	
B. 6 oz. Round P. W. M. (high, square shoulder)	9 00
8 oz. Round Pres. W. M.	
H. 8 oz. Round Pres. W. M. (high)	10 50
B. 8 oz. Round Pres. W. M. (horse radish)	
12 oz. Round Pres. W. M.	13 00

OVALS, UNION OVALS, PHILADELPHIA OVALS.

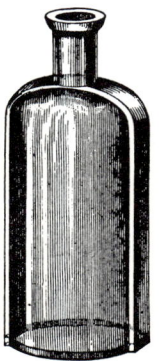
Union Oval.

Philadelphia Oval.

	Per Gross.
½ oz.	$3 25
1 oz. and long 1 oz.	3 75
1¾ oz.	} 4 75
2 oz. and long 2 oz.	
3 oz.	5 75
3½ oz.	} 7 00
4 oz.	
S. 6 oz. (small)	} 8 50
L. 6 oz. (large)	
S. 8 oz. (small)	} 10 25
H. 8 oz. (high)	
L. 8 oz. (large)	
10 oz. (Philadelphia Oval)	13 00
12 oz.	14 25
14 oz.	15 75
L. Pt. (large)	} 17 50
F. 16 oz. (flat)	
L. & S. Quart	25 00

PANELS.

	Per gross.
½ oz.	$3 50
T. 5 and 6 drachm	} 4 00
S. 1 oz. (small)	
L. 1 oz. (large)	
1¼ & S. 1½ oz.	
1½ oz.	
S. 2 oz. (small)	} 5 50
L. 2 oz. (large)	
P. 2 oz. (plain on one side)	
Balt. P. 2 oz. (" ")	} 5 50
Tall 2 oz. (plain on one side)	
S. 3 oz. (small)	
P. 3 oz. (plain on one side)	
H. 3 oz. (high)	} 7 00
Tall 3 oz. (plain on one side)	
H. 4 oz. (high)	
P. 4 oz. (plain on one side)	} 8 00
Tall 4 oz. (plain on one side)	

8 oz. Tall.

PANELS—Continued.

	Per gross.
5 oz.	$9 25
S. 6 oz. (small)	
L. 6 oz. (large)	} 10 50
P. 6 oz. (plain on one side)	
Tall 6 oz. (plain on one side)	
H. 8 oz. (high)	
P. 8 oz. (plain on one side)	} 13 00
Tall 8 oz. (plain on one side)	
10 oz.	15 50
B. 12 oz. (broad, plain on one side)	} 17 50
H. 12 oz (high)	
14 oz.	18 75
16 oz.	
B. 16 oz. (broad, plain on one side)	} 21 00
24 oz.	26 00

Ball Neck Panel.

For Plates for lettering most of the above, see page 9.

BULB OR BALL-NECK PANELS, 2 ounce and under, 50 cents per gross advance on the above prices. Over 2 ounce, $1.00 per gross.

COD LIVER OILS AND LONG NECK PANELS.

1½ oz. Baltimore	$6 00
2 oz.	6 00
3 oz. Baltimore	7 50
4 oz. and Baltimore 4 oz.	8 50
7 oz.	12 50
8 oz. and Baltimore 8 oz.	13 50
12 oz.	18 50
16 oz.	21 50

Cod Liver. For Plates for lettering, see page 9.

CASTOR OILS. I. M., OR LEMON SYRUPS.

1⅞ oz., T. 2 oz. and L. 2 oz.	$5 25
2½ oz.	} 5 75
3 oz.	
4 oz.	6 75
5 oz.	7 50
6 oz.	8 25
7 oz.	9 25
8 oz.	10 50
9 oz.	11 00
10 oz.	12 00
12 oz.	13 25
13 oz.	14 25
14 oz. (and N. Y. Style)	15 00
16 oz.	16 00
18 oz.	18 00
20 oz.	21 00
22 oz.	23 00
Pt. Lemon Syrup (9½ oz.)	12 00
6 oz. Flat C. Oils	10 00

GREEN GLASSWARE.

OVAL AND FLUTED CASTOR OILS, Etc.

	Per Gross.
2 oz. OVAL C. OIL (called ¼ Pt.)	$5 50
4 oz. OVAL C. OIL (called ½ Pt.)	8 00
8 oz. OVAL C. OIL (called Pint)	11 00
16 oz. OVAL C. OIL (called Qt.)	19 00
8 oz. FLUTED C. OIL	11 00
16 oz. FLUTED C. OIL	17 00
6 oz. OCTAGON FLAT OIL, Long Neck, or ½ Pint Rose Water	10 00

Oval Castor Oil.

FRENCH SQUARES, BLAKES & OCTAGONS.
(For other styles French Squares see Page 13.)

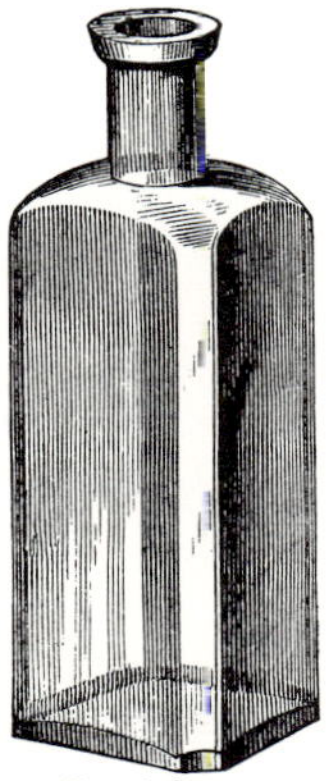

	Per Gross.
½ oz. and 1 oz.	$4 00
1¼ oz. and 2 oz.	5 00
2½ oz. and 3 oz.	} 6 25
S. 3 oz. (Octagon)	
4 oz.	7 50
5 oz.	8 50
6 oz.	9 50
8 oz.	11 75
10 oz.	14 00
12 oz.	16 00
14 oz.	17 25
16 oz.	19 25
24 oz.	26 00
32 oz.	31 00
2 oz. Octagon, L. Neck	5 50

French Square.

TALL BLAKES (English Style) 1, 2, 3, 4, 6, 8 & 10 oz.

For Plates for lettering see Page 8.

PATENT MEDICINES AND OTHER VIALS.

	Per Gross.
HARLEM OILS	
PEPPERMINT	
TURLINGTON'S	} $3 75
LEMON ACIDS	
BRITISH OILS	
BATEMAN'S	
GENUINE ESSENCE and PLAIN	} 4 00
DALBY'S CARMINATIVE	
GODFREY'S CORDIAL	
Liquid and Demi OPODELDOCS	
STEER'S OPO'S, L. & S.	
CEPHALIC SNUFF	} 4 50
BALSAM HONEY	
OX MARROWS (Round & Sq.)	
PRESTON SALTS	
Flat BEAR'S Oil and Small do.	
Large BEAR'S Oil	
Flat BALSAM	} 4 75
CAYENNES	
CALC. MAGNESIA	

Flat Bear's Oil.

SELTZERS OR PACKING BOTTLES, Common Weight.
NARROW MOUTH.

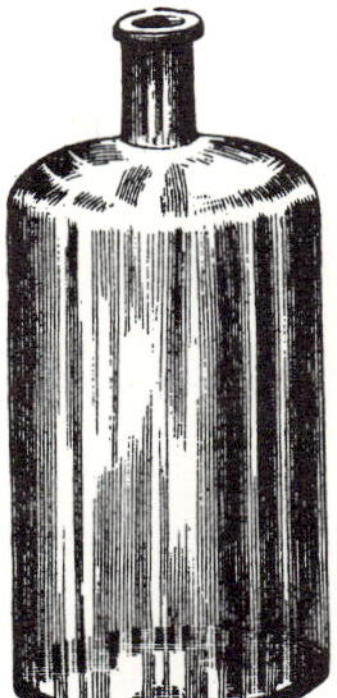

	Per Gross.
½ Pint	$9 75
14 oz.	} 15 25
1 Pint	
1½ Pint	19 50
Quart	24 50
3 Pint	32 75
½ Gallon	39 00
3 Quart	44 00
1 Gallon	56 00

WIDE MOUTH.

	Per Gross.
14 oz. Seltzer	} 16 25
B. S. Pt. Seltz. & Pt. Selt.	
C. 20 oz.	20 50
1½ Pt. Selt. or ¼ ℔. Mag.	20 50
Quart Seltzer	25 50
3 Pint or ½ ℔. Magnesia	33 75
½ Gallon Seltzer	40 00
3 Quart or 1 ℔. Magnesia	45 00
1 Gallon	57 00

EXTRA SELTZERS.
NARROW MOUTH.
Extra Size and Weight.

	Per Gross.
½ Pint and 9 oz.	$12 25
12 oz.	15 00
Pint, 18 oz. to 20 oz.	19 50
22 oz. to 1½ Pint, and 24 oz.	24 00
Quart, 35 oz.	30 00
3 Pint	40 00
½ Gallon, 80 oz. (5 pints)	55 00
3 Quart	63 00
1 Gallon	70 00
2 Gallon	170 00

WIDE MOUTH.
Extra Size and Weight.

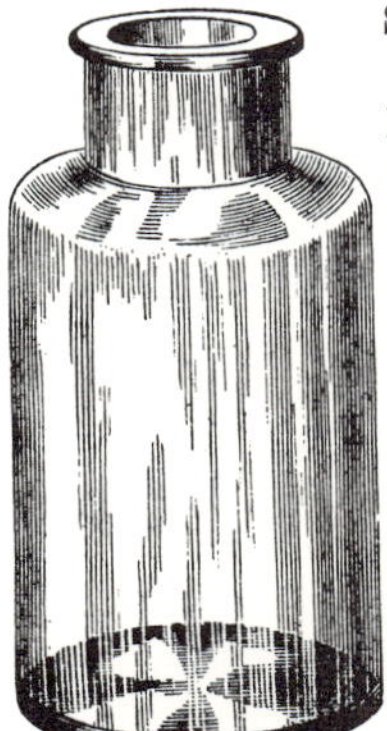

	Per Gross.
S. ½ Pt. Seltzer, or Charcoal Bottle	
M. ½ Pint Seltzer	} $13 25
L. ½ Pint Seltzer	
12 oz.	16 00
14 oz.	18 00
Pt. and C. Pt. & 19 oz. W. M.	} 20 50
20 oz.	
1½ Pint	25 00
Quart	31 00
3 Pint	41 00
½ Gallon	56 00
3 Quart	64 00
Gallon	71 00
2 Gallon	171 00

4

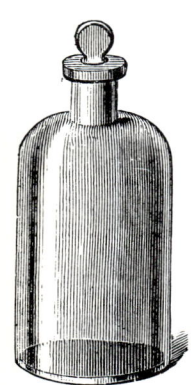

ACIDS.
Dark Green.

We call attention to the high reputation over the United States of our Stoppered Acids, and invite comparison in elegance of make and tightness of stoppering, with those produced elsewhere.

	Per Gross.
½ Pint, Ground Stoppers	$30 00
10 oz., Ground Stoppers	32 50
12 oz., Ground Stoppers	34 00
1 Pint, Ground Stoppers	36 00
1 Quart, Ground Stoppers	48 00
½ Gallon, Ground Stoppers	75 00
1 Gallon, Ground Stoppers	96 00
2 Gallon, Ground Stoppers	210 00
Chloride of Soda, or Stoppered Wines	42 00

ENGLISH ESSENTIAL OILS.
Extra Seltzers, High Shape, Dark Green.
(For Blue Style, see page 19.)
(For Flint Style, see page 18.)

	Per Gross.	
	For Corks.	Stoppered.
½ Pint	$12 75	$30 00
Pint	20 50	36 00
Quart	31 50	48 00
½ Gallon	58 60	75 00

NURSING BOTTLES.
(See Cuts, Page 17.)

	Per Gross.
Infant's, Straight Neck	$12 00
Empire, Bent Neck	} 14 00
Acme, Bent Neck and Round Bottom	
Millville, No. 1 (Narrow, for Nipples)	} 12 00
Millville, No. 2 (Wide, for Fittings)	
Baltimore	10 50
12 oz., Flask	18 00

PROMISCUOUS ARTICLES.

	Per Gross.
Citrate Magnesia, 9 oz.	12 00
Citrate Magnesia, 12 oz.	17 75
Citrate Magnesia, 12 oz. Lett'd Mould	17 75
1 Pound Calomels	8 75
Plain Oldridges, 6 oz.	7 75
Glycerine	15 00
Glycerine Stoppers	3 75
Pint Caustics	16 25
4 oz. Oval Ginger	7 00
Florida Water, 3½ oz. Plain	6 75
Florida Water, Large. Plain	} 12 00
Florida Water, Large. Lettered	
Florida Water, Small. Lettered	
Rose Waters, ½ Pint	10 00

Varnish.

	Per Gross.
Rose Water, 1 Pint	15 00
4 oz. Round Yeast Powder	6 75
6 oz. Round Yeast Powder	8 25
Sponge Blacking or Varnish	8 00
Cottin-a-Paris, small	7 25
Cottin-a-Paris, large	11 00
½ Pint Paint Jars	12 50
4 oz. N. Y. Paint Jars	9 50
8 oz. N. Y. Paint Jars	12 50
Insect Powder, 3 oz.	5 75

Paint Jar.

INK BOTTLES.

	Per Gross.
Indelible	$3 75
Mordant	4 00
Red	3 75
1 oz.	3 75
2 oz.	4 00
4 oz.	5 50
4 oz. Pour Out	7 00
6 oz.	8 00
8 oz.	9 50
8 oz. Pour Out	11 00
Pint	15 75
Pint, Pour Out	17 25
C. Quart	} 22 00
O. S. Quart, Short Neck	
C. Quart, O. S. and Pour Out	23 50

INK STANDS.

B. 2 oz. Ink.

Fluted Pyramid Ink.

Fluted Fountain Ink.

	Per Gross
1 oz. F. Pyramid	4 00
2 oz. F. Pyramid	5 50
2 oz. Flat Inks	5 50
B. 2 oz. Inks, no lips, teapot	4 75
L. Teapot	4 75
2 oz. Plain Fountain	4 75
2 oz. Fluted Fountain	4 75
1 oz. Cone Carmine	4 25
½ oz. Round Ink	3 50

SQUARE CARMINE INKS.

	Per gross.
½ oz.	$3 50
1 oz.	4 00
2 oz.	5 00
4 oz.	7 50
5 oz.	8 50
8 oz.	12 00

MUCILAGE.

	Per Gross.
Pint P. O.	17 25
Quart P. O.	23 50
2¼ oz. Cone	
3 oz. Cone	} 6 00
3 oz. N.Y.	
8 oz. Cone	13 50
8 oz. Flat	17 00

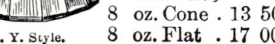
N. Y. Style.

Cone Style.

MIXED WARE.

At the Same Discount as other Green Glass.

PEPPER SAUCE.

Fluted Pepper Sauce.

Tomato C. Flask.

Square Gothic.

	Per gross.
Plain Round, Pint	$11 50
Plain Round, Quart	17 00
Fluted Round, Pint	12 00
Fluted Round, Quart	17 50
Square Gothic, Pint	12 25
Square Gothic, Quart	17 75
Hexagon, Pint	12 25
Hexagon, Quart	17 75
Tomato Catsup Flasks, Quart	17 75
Tomato Catsup Flasks, Pint	11 75
Tomato Catsup Flasks, S. Pint	10 75

MUSTARDS, &c.

	Per gross.
Pound	$19 00
Half pound	12 50
Quarter pound, flat	7 50
Quarter pound, square	7 00
London	7 00
Barrel Mustards	9 00
Square Horse Radish	9 25
Hexagon Horse Radish	9 50
6 oz. Round Horse Radish	9 00
Round Horse Radish, 8 oz (or B. 8 oz., W. M.)	10 50

SNUFFS.

	Per Gross.
½ pound Maccouba	$12 00
Pound Maccouba	17 50
½ pound, Scotch	12 00

JELLIES OR PRESERVE JARS.

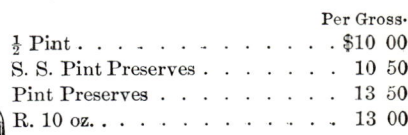

	Per Gross.
½ Pint	$10 00
S. S. Pint Preserves	10 50
Pint Preserves	13 50
R. 10 oz.	13 00

CLUB SAUCE.

	Per Gross.
½ Pint Club Sauce	$9 50
Pint Club Sauce	13 75
Sauce Stoppers, Large & H.	3 75
Sauce Stoppers, Small	3 75

Club Sauce.

PICKLE JARS.

	Per Gross.
S. Pint, 8 oz. weight (Batty Style)	$13 00
Pint, 10¼ oz. weight (Batty Style)	15 50
S. Qt., 13½ oz. weight (Batty Style)	19 00
Quart, 14½ oz. weight (Batty Style)	20 50
S. ½ gal., 20 oz. weight (Batty Style)	30 00
½ Gal., 23 oz. weight, (Batty Style)	33 00
Gallon, 44 oz. weight, (Batty Style)	61 00
Round Pint, 13½ oz. weight	19 50
Round Pint, 15 oz. weight	21 00
Round Q'rt, 15½ oz. weight (Shaker Style)	23 50
Pint Gothic, 10 oz. weight	15 00
Pint Gothic, 13 oz. weight	18 00
Gallon Hexagon P. Jars	61 00

BRANDY FRUITS, &c.

	Per Gross
½ Pint	$11 50
1½ Pint	16 25
Brandy Cherries	23 50
½ Pint, (Fancy French)	11 50
Pint, (F'cy French)	17 50
½ Pint, Sweet Oils, foot	10 00
Pint, Sweet Oils, foot	13 00

Brandy Fruit.

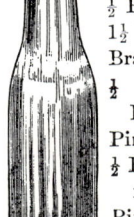
Fancy French.

MINERALS.

	Per Gross.
Green, 13 oz. in weight	$17 75
Green, 14 oz. in weight	13 75
Green, 15 oz. in weight	19 75
Green, 16 oz. in weight	22 00

DARK WINE BOTTLES.

	Per Gross.
5 to Gallon	$25 00
5½ to Gallon	24 50
6 to Gallon & S. 6	22 75
7 to Gallon	21 50
8 to Gallon	19 00
10 to Gallon	15 00

AMBER SCHNAPPS.

	Per Gross.
Pint, 12 to 13 oz. weight	$17 75
Pint, 13 to 14 oz. weight	18 75
6 to Gallon, 19 oz. weight	25 50
5 to Gallon, 21 oz. weight	27 75

PLAIN FRUIT JARS, For Corks.

	Per Gross.
Pint	$18 50
Quart	24 25
Half Gallon	38 50

HONEY JARS.

	Per Gross.
Small size, 8 oz. content	$11 50
Small size, 8 oz. content, extra weight	14 00
Large size, 10 oz. content	12 50
Square Pint Pickle Jars (for Honey)	14 00
Short Wedge Panel Honey	20 00
Maple Syrup, extra weight	23 50

HAND-MADE BOTTLES.

	Per Dozen.
Quart	$2 00
Half Gallon	3 50

CARBOYS.

	Each.
10 Gallon, Naked	$3 00
12 Gallon, "	3 50

DEMIJOHNS, Covered.

	Per Dozen.
Quart	
½ Gallon	
Gallon	
2 Gallon	
3 Gallon	
5 Gallon	

INSULATORS, BATTERY JARS, Etc., Etc.

The Millville Atmospheric Fruit Jar.

The jar has been in use for a series of years, with steadily increasing satisfaction. During this period many new varieties of Jars for preserving fruit have been introduced, but after one or two seasons' trial many of them have been abandoned as worthless, while the reputation of the Millville Jar has constantly increased. The owners confidently refer to the houses who have handled it for so many seasons, as to the full satisfaction it has given to their customers.

IT IS SOLD WITHOUT LIMIT OF PRICE AS TO RE-SALE.

No Claim has ever been made upon it, on account of Infringing other Patents.

The high standard of quality and workmanship heretofore uniformly maintained in the manufacture of this Jar will be fully sustained in the future.

It possesses the following ADVANTAGES in addition to those of the Ring Jar.

I. A heavier pressure can probably be put on a screw with a fine thread like that of the Millville than that of any ring jar.

II. It is a Test Jar. After the fruit is put up and allowed to cool, the clamp can be removed, and by trying the lid it can be ascertained whether the joint is tight and a vacuum inside. If this is not the case, the fruit can be heated over at once, and thus saved from spoiling.

III. The Clamps are made of malleable iron, so that if too great force is applied in screwing they will yield under great pressure, and come off the jar, without injuring either it or themselves.

IV. The lids are made very thick and strong where the pressure of the screw comes upon them, so that they will rarely, if ever, break in this way.

DRUGGISTS' SUNDRIES

LARGELY

OF OUR OWN

MANUFACTURE.

₊*₊ In ordering Glassware please look through our Sundry List and send for wants in this line.

DRUGGISTS' SUNDRIES.
AT NET PRICES.

We have added to our business the manufacture and sale of a superior grade of DRUGGISTS' SUNDRIES. We hope to maintain in this department the character for superior workmanship and quality which has been kindly accorded us by those who have for forty years used our Glassware.

We solicit a trial of the quality and price of these goods by our numerous customers. We keep a stock on hand both in our New York and Philadelphia houses, and are also prepared to furnish any standard goods not on our list at current prices.

Price List.—Net.

NURSING BOTTLES.
COMPLETE WITH FITTINGS.
PER DOZEN. ONE DOZEN IN BOX.

Acme Nursing Bottle.

FLINT GLASS.

For FITTINGS, see page 54.	Valve Crystal. Extra Quality Fittings.	Crystal Black Fittings.	Patent Valve Black Fittings.	Enamel. Black Fittings	Plain White Fittings.
THE ACME	$2 10	$1 70	$2 10	$1 70	$1 45
THE EMPIRE	2 10	1 70	2 10	1 70	1 45
The same as the ACME, but with flat bottom.					
THE INFANTS	2 00	1 60	2 00	1 60	1 35
THE MILLVILLE	2 00	1 60	2 00	1 60	1 35
See Cut page 53.					

GREEN GLASS.

THE ACME		1 90	1 50	1 90	1 50	1 25
THE EMPIRE		1 90	1 50	1 90	1 50	1 25
THE INFANTS		1 80	1 40	1 80	1 40	1 15
THE MILLVILLE,		1 80	1 40	1 80	1 40	1 15

Each in neat separate box with Tube and Bottle Brushes, One Dollar extra per dozen.

For Lettered Plates for Nursing Bottles see Page 17.

NURSING BOTTLES, COMPLETE, WITH VALVE CRYSTAL FITTINGS.

We ask the attention of the Trade to our VALVE CRYSTAL FITTING for Nursing Bottles.

The Vent in Stopper, closed by a self-acting valve, allows the outside air to enter the bottle as fast as the milk is taken out, thereby insuring a perfectly easy and steady flow of milk, and at the same time allows no milk to escape by the valve.

Nursing bottles, with the Valve Crystal Fittings, can be filled with milk and carried, when traveling, without danger of leakage, and are always ready for use.

AT NET PRICES.

ONE DOZEN IN BOX.

	Per Dozen.			Per Dozen.	
	Black Rubber.	White Rubber.		Black Rubber.	White Rubber.
THE PHENIX, Bent Neck, FLINT, each in Paper Box with brushes,	$3 10	$3 00	THE ACME, Bent Neck, Round Bottom, GREEN	1 90	1 80
THE EMPIRE, (same shape), FLINT,	2 10	2 00	THE INFANTS, Straight Neck, FLINT,	2 00	1 90
THE EMPIRE, (same shape), GREEN,	1 90	1 80	THE INFANTS, Straight Neck, GREEN,	1 80	1 70
THE ACME, Bent Neck, R'd Bottom, FLINT	2 10	2 00	THE MILLVILLE, (see cut), FLINT,	2 00	1 90
			THE MILLVILLE, (see cut), GREEN,	1 80	1 70

NURSING BOTTLES, WITHOUT FITTINGS.

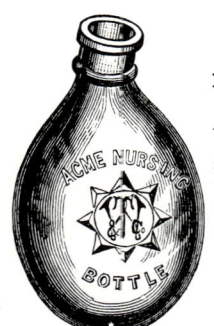

The Acme.

THE ACME.
Bent Neck. Round Bottom.

Being without corners, this bottle is more easily cleansed and kept sweet than any other. When laid on the side, the mouth is elevated above the contents of the bottle.

	Per Doz.
FLINT	$ 70
GREEN	50

THE EMPIRE.
Bent Neck. Straight Bottom.

The Bent Neck is of great advantage in self-feeding.

FLINT	70
GREEN	50

THE INFANTS.
Straight Neck and Bottom.

FLINT	60
GREEN	40

Infant's.

THE MILLVILLE.
Adapted for Grasping.

	Per Doz.
FLINT, No. 1, Nar'w Mouth for Nipples, FLINT, No. 2, Wide Mouth for Fittings,	60
GREEN, No. 1, Nar'w Mouth for Nipples, GREEN, No. 2, Wide Mouth for Fittings,	40

BALTIMORE NURSING FLASK.
Narrow Mouth for Nipples.

FLINT	55
GREEN	35

12 OUNCE NURSING FLASK.

FLINT	90
GREEN	60

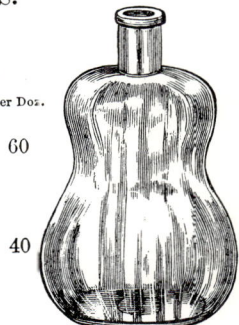

Millville.

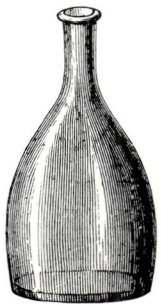

Baltimore.

NURSING BOTTLE FITTINGS
OF SUPERIOR MATERIAL.
At Net Prices.

FITTINGS.

UNIVERSAL MAROON.

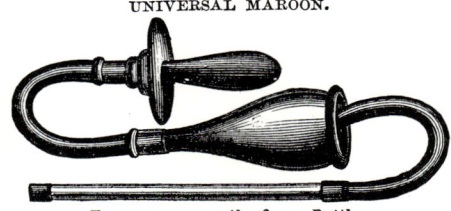

To go over mouth of any Bottle.

	Per Gross.
Extra Quality, Ivory Guards	$18 00

UNIVERSAL, PATENT VALVE.

	Per Gross.
White Rubber	16 00

CRYSTAL.

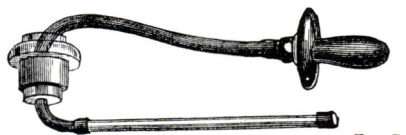

	Per Gross.
Black Rubber, complete	12 00

The Stoppers are of Flint glass, so that contact with the milk is almost wholly glass. The connectors and guards are of fine French Jet.

VALVE CRYSTAL.

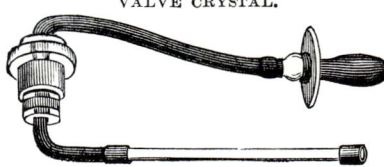

Below the closing of the mouth a VENT is pierced in the Glass and covered by a rubber valve, which allows the air to enter the bottle as the milk is withdrawn, but entirely prevents the milk from leaking through the vent. It is greatly superior to the valve at the top of the stopper.

	Per Gross.
Best Quality MAROON, Ivory Guard, complete	16 50

PATENT VALVE.

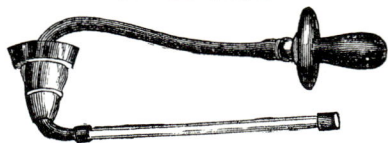

	Per Gross.
BLACK, complete	16 50
WHITE, complete	15 50

BLACK RUBBER.
	Per Gross.
With ENAMEL FINISH Guard	12 00

WHITE RUBBER.
	Per Gross.
PLAIN, with WHITE TOPS	9 00

NIPPLES.

PLAIN.

Nipple.

	Per Gross.	
	Black.	White.
SMALL	$2 80	$1 80
MEDIUM	3 30	2 40
LARGE	4 60	3 80

	Per Gross.
MAROON, Medium	3 50
CORK or PLUG, White	8 00

PATENT VALVE.

	Per Gross.
Black	4 20
White	3 00

DAVIDSON'S.

Davidson's.

	Per Gross.
No. 26, Black	5 70
No. 22, White	5 00

SWAN BILL.

	Per Gross.
MAROON, 1 dozen in box	2 80
MAROON, Large. Not boxed	2 80

Swan Bill.   Swan Bill, No. 2.   Swan Bill, No. 8.

	Per Gross.	
	Black.	White.
"Swan Bill"	2 40	1 80
Swan Bill, No. 2	3 00	2 40
Swan Bill, No. 8	3 60	3 00

INSECT POWDER GUNS.

	Per Gross.
White Rubber	9 00

SUNDRIES.
AT NET PRICES.

RUBBER TUBING.

	Per Foot.	Per ℔.
Black, ⅛ inch	$ 05	$3 30
Maroon, ⅛ inch	05	3 30
White, ⅛ inch	04	1 50

	Per Gross.
Black Rubber for Fittings, 8 inch	6 00
Maroon Rubber for Fittings, 8 inch,	6 00
White Rubber for Fittings, 8 inch,	4 80

GLASS TUBES.
	Per Gross.
For Fittings	1 20

BRUSHES.
For Nursing Bottles	3 00
For Tubes	1 80
THE PERFECT CLEANER	12 00

TEETHING PADS, RINGS AND SHIELDS.
TEETHING PADS ON CARDS.
	Per Doz.
Maroon or Black Rubber	1 00
White Rubber	75
White Corrugated	90

TEETHING RINGS.
	Per Doz.
Black Rubber	75
White Rubber	50
White Corrugated	60

BREAST SHIELDS
1 DOZ. IN BOX.
	Per Doz.
Black Rubber	80
White Rubber	60

PHENIX NIPPLE SHIELDS AND SHELLS.
	Per Dozen.
Glass, with FLEXIBLE TUBE, (in box)	1 75
Glass, with NIPPLE AND IVORY SHIELD, (in box)	1 25
GLASS NIPPLE SHELLS	75
Glass NIPPLE SHELL, with loop for suspending round the neck	85
FRENCH JET NIPPLE SHIELDS	1 00

BREAST PUMPS.
	Per Doz.
PHENIX, with Rubber Bulb (in box)	$4 00
PHENIX, with Flexible Tube (in box)	2 50

LEECH TUBES.
BENT	60
STRAIGHT	60

CUPPING GLASSES.
CUPPING GLASSES	1 00
CUPPING GLASSES, with Rubber Bulb	3 00

RUBBER BULBS.
For BREAST PUMPS, heavy	2 50
For SYRINGES, SINGLE NECK	2 00
DOUBLE NECK	3 00

FINGER COTS.
	Per Gross.
White, heavy	4 50
White, extra heavy	6 25
Black	5 25
Black, heavy	7 25
Black, extra heavy	8 50

EAR CLEANERS.
	Per Dozen.
Plated Wire Handles	75
Bone Handles	1 50

PROBANGS.
	Per Gross
Whalebone,	12 00
Whalebone, Ivory Tip	15 00
Whalebone, Imitation,	6 75
Wire	9 00

MISCELLANEOUS.
AT NET PRICES.

FOUNTAIN NASAL DOUCHE.

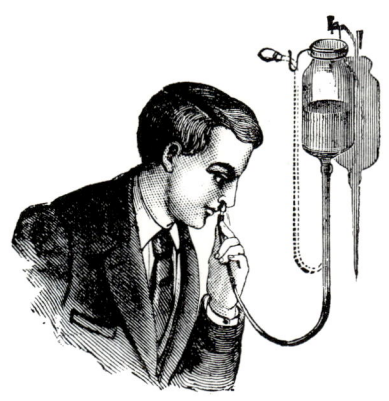

12 OUNCE GLASS RESERVOIR.
With rubber tubing and improved glass end.

	Per Doz.
In box	$4 50
Extra glass ends	36

One wire hook suspends it to the wall, and another supports the nasal piece above the water level when not in use. It is considered the most cleanly and convenient Douche offered to purchasers.

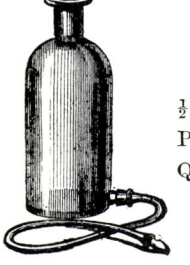

NASAL DOUCHES.
With Rubber Tubes. Each Douche in Box.

	Per Doz.
½ Pint	$5 50
Pint	6 00
Quart	6 50

HYDROKONION.

	Per Doz.
Hydrokonion	$4 50

POCKET INHALING TUBE.

	Per Doz.
All Glass, each in box	$1 50
1 dozen in box	1 00

GLASS NASAL SYRINGE.

Jet top, Colored Piston	1 25

NASAL POWDER DOUCHE.

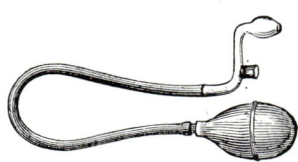

The Powder is placed in opening in side of tube, which is then closed by the finger or by a cork and the Powder is blown through the nose-piece, at end of glass tube.

	Per Doz.
Each in box	$5 00

MEDICINE DROPPERS.

	Per Doz.
All Glass	1 25

FRENCH PIPETTES—Rubber Bulb.
On Cards of 1 dozen each.

BENT.

STRAIGHT.

EXACT.

The exact are carefully adjusted so as to give nearly as can be the standard pharmaceutical drop.

	Per Doz.
BENT	50
STRAIGHT	50
EXACT	50

MEDICINE TUBES—All Glass.
BENT AND STRAIGHT.

	Per Gross.
8 inches long	1 25
10 inches long	1 75
Assorted Colors, 10 inches long	2 25

GRUEL TUBES—All Glass.
VERY HEAVY, BENT.

	Per Gross.
⅜ x 12 inches	4 00

STIRRING RODS.

	Per Doz.
8 inch length	50
12 inch length	75

SYRINGES.
AT NET PRICES.

THE HOUSEHOLD.

With *Rubber Connections* and *French Jet Pipes*, not liable to rust and non-conductors of heat. *Valves* secured in the centre bulb, rendering their loss impossible.

	Per Dozen.
No. 1. 4 Pipes	$12 50
No. 2. 3 Pipes	8 67
No. 3. 2 Pipes	6 50

THE ACME.

Nickel Plated Pipes, with *Rubber Connections*. *Valves secured*, as in Household.

	Per Dozen.
No. 1. 4 Pipes	$10 50
No. 2. 3 Pipes	5 50
No. 3. 2 Pipes	4 00
MATTSON'S IMPROVED, in Wooden Box, Bulb in centre, 3 Pipes	10 50
IMPERIAL, in Paper Box, Bulb in centre, 3 Pipes	5 50
SEASIDE, in Paper Box, Bulb in centre, 2 Pipes	4 00
ANCHOR, in Wooden Box, 3 Pipes	6 00
PHENIX, No. 1, in Wooden Box, Nickel Plated, 5 Pipes	10 00

PHENIX—Paper Box.

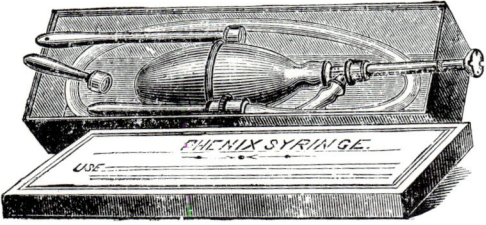

	Per Dozen.
Nickel Plated, 2 pipes	$3 50
Nickel Plated, 3 pipes	4 00

WHITE METAL SYRINGES.
DOUBLE LEATHER PISTON.

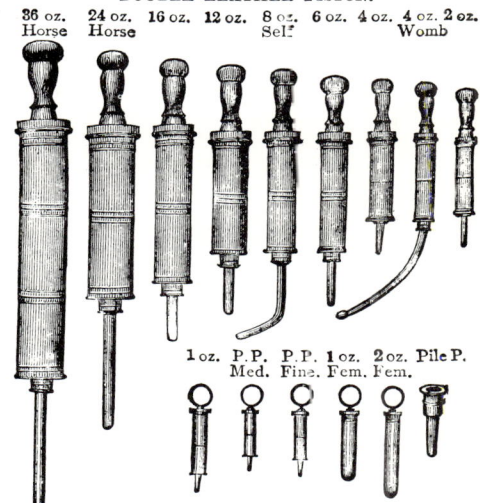

36 oz. Horse   24 oz. Horse   16 oz.   12 oz.   8 oz. Self.   6 oz.   4 oz.   4 oz. 2 oz. Womb

1 oz. P. P. Med.   P. P. Fine.   1 oz. Fem.   2 oz. Fem.   Pile P.

	Per Dozen.	
	Fine.	Medium.
24 oz. self, in wood case, 2 pipes	$30 00	$25 00
16 oz. self, in wood case	21 00	16 00
12 oz. self, in wood case	18 00	14 00
10 oz. self, in wood case	15 00	12 00
8 oz. self, in wood case	14 00	11 00
6 oz. self, in wood case	12 00	9 00
4 oz. self, in wood case	9 00	7 00
24 oz. single, in paper boxes	24 00	18 00
16 oz. single, in paper boxes	16 00	12 00
12 oz. single, in paper boxes	12 00	10 00
10 oz. single, in paper boxes	10 00	9 00
8 oz. single, in paper boxes	9 00	7 00
6 oz. single, in paper boxes	7 00	5 00
4 oz. single, in paper boxes	5 00	4 00
2 oz. single, in paper boxes	4 00	3 00
1 oz. single, in paper boxes	3 00	2 50
½ oz. or P. P. fine	1 50	1 00
1 oz. Female, fine	2 50	1 75
2 oz. Female, fine	3 00	2 00
4 oz. Female, fine	3 50	
2 oz. Womb, 2 pipes, in case	9 00	6 00
4 oz. Womb, 2 pipes, in case	12 00	7 00
6 oz. Womb, 2 pipes, in case	11 00	9 00
1 oz. Ear Syr., ivory pipe in handle	6 00	

HORSE SYRINGES.

	Per Dozen.
24 oz. in case	$30 00
36 oz. in case	36 00
48 oz. in case	48 00
	Each.
Horse Pump, (metal) large size	$7 00

SYRINGES.

GLASS, WITH FRENCH JET CAPS AND COLORED PISTONS.
1 Dozen in Box.

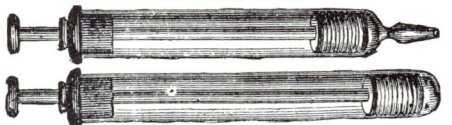

Glass of extra weight and Annealed. French Points, and smoothed ends. Our Best Style.

	Per Gross. Male.	Female.
No. 00	$8 00	
No. 0	9 00	
No. 1	10 50	
No. 2	12 00	
No. 3	14 00	15 00
No. 4	18 00	18 00
No. 5		21 00
No. 6		27 00
No. 7		32 00

ALL GLASS.

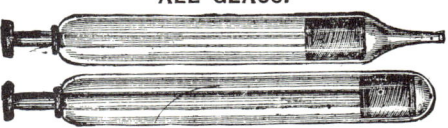

Extra Weight.

GLASS, FITTED WITH CORKS.
Extra Weight. Annealed.

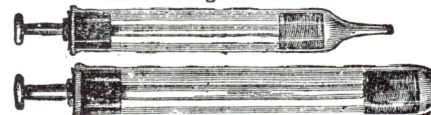

The Pistons can be removed and the packing renewed should it wear out.

	All Glass. Per Gross. Male.	Female.	Fitted with Corks. Per Gross. Male.	Female.
No. 00	$8 00		$8 00	
No. 0	9 00		9 00	
No. 1	10 50	12 00	10 50	12 00
No. 2	12 00	13 50	12 00	13 50
No. 3	14 00	15 00	14 00	15 00
No. 4	18 00	18 00	18 00	18 00
No. 5	21 00	21 00	21 00	21 00
No. 6	27 00	27 00	27 00	27 00

GLASS—RUBBER CAP.

	Per Gross.
PEERLESS, No. 1, Urethral	$20 00
PEERLESS, No. 2, same as No. 3, but larger	22 00
PEERLESS, No. 3, Ear and Nasal	20 00
PEERLESS, No. 4, same as No. 3, but larger	22 00
PEERLESS, No. 5, same as No. 1, Hard Rubber Tip	27 00
PEERLESS, No. 6, same as No. 2, Hard Rubber Tip	30 00

GLASS, WITH FRENCH JET PISTONS.
1 Dozen in Box.

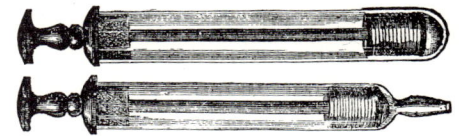

Glass of extra weight and Annealed. French Points and smoothed ends.

	Per Gross. Male.	Female.
No. 0	$8 00	
No. 1	9 00	
No. 2	10 00	
No. 3	12 00	12 50
No. 4		14 00
No. 5		18 00
No. 6		25 00
No. 7		30 00

PATENT CAP.
GLASS, WITH METAL CAPS.

	Per Gross. Male.	Female.
No. 0	$8 00	
No. 1	9 00	10 00
No. 2	10 00	11 00
No. 3	12 00	12 50
No. 4	14 00	14 00
No. 5	18 00	18 00
No. 6	25 00	25 00
No. 7	30 00	30 00

GLASS IN WOOD CASE.
FRENCH JET CAPS. COLORED PISTONS.

	Per Gross. Male.
No. 00	$10 00
No. 0	11 00
No. 1	13 00

	All Glass. Per Gross. Male.	Female.	Patent Cap. Per Gross. Male.
No. 00	$10 00	$11 50	$10 50
No. 0	11 00	12 50	12 00
No. 1	13 00	14 50	14 25
No. 2	15 00	16 50	

FRENCH JET.

A substitute for Hard Rubber, in a material not liable to rust, and a non-conductor of heat and cold. Warranted not to swell in water.

	Per Dozen.
MALE, No. 1	$3 25
MALE, No. 10	2 60
FEMALE, No. 2	4 50
FEMALE, No. 3	5 50

SYRINGES.
AT NET PRICES.

COMBINATION POCKET.
Glass Bottle, with Metal Cap and Glass Syringe combined.

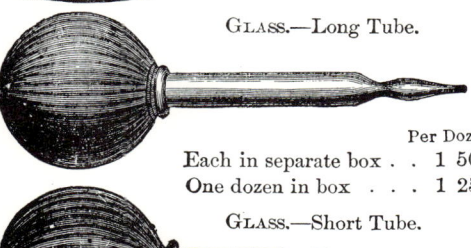

	Per Doz.
Each in Box, 2 oz.	$2 50
Each in Box, 4 oz.	3 00

P. P. BULB.
NICKEL PLATED.

	Per Doz.
Each in separate box	2 00

GLASS.—Long Tube.

	Per Doz.
Each in separate box	1 50
One dozen in box	1 25

GLASS.—Short Tube.

	Per Doz.
Each in separate box	1 50
One dozen in box	1 25

GLASS FOUNTAIN.
1½ Pint Reservoir for hanging on wall or frame of door. With a hook at top of Reservoir to rest the pipe on when not in use. It is not liable to corrosion by acids. The force of injection is regulated by the height at which the Reservoir is hung, and the stream is steady. The flow is stopped by a clasp on the rubber. This is the most cleanly and pleasant form of Syringe now in use.

	Per Doz.
In Box, with Four heavy Glass Pipes, Two Pipes of Metal, Nickel Plated, Six Feet of Tubing and Sprinkler	12 00

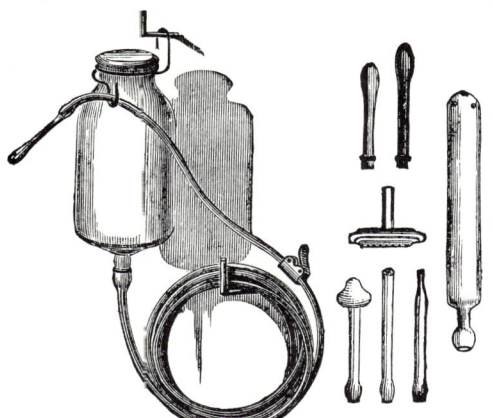

EYE OR DENTAL SYRINGE.

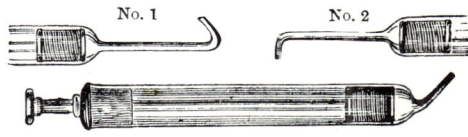
No. 1   No. 2

No. 3

	Per Doz.
GLASS, JET TOP AND COLORED PISTON	1 25

BULB EYE BATH.

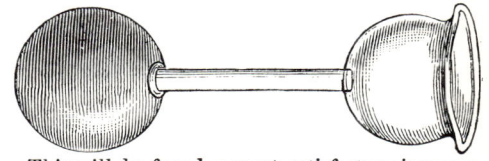

This will be found a most satisfactory improvement for bathing the eye.

	Per Doz.
Each in box	$2 00

FLUTED EYE BATHS.

	Per Doz.
Fluted Eye Baths	1 50

GLASS EAR SYRINGES.

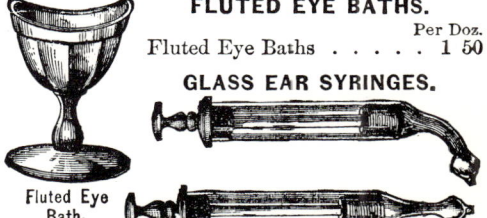
Fluted Eye Bath.

FRENCH JET TOPS AND PATENT CAP.
1 Dozen in Box.

	French Jet Tops. Per Gross.	Patent Cap. Per Gross.
Bent	15 00	15 00
Straight	15 00	15 00

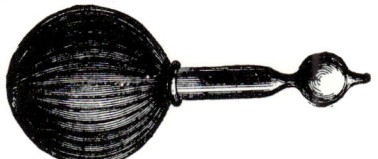

EAR BULB SYRINGES.
GLASS TUBES.

	Per Gross.
Each in separate box	18 00
One dozen in box	15 00

SUPPOSITORY SYRINGES.

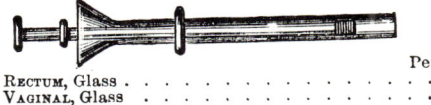

	Per Doz.
RECTUM, Glass	1 50
VAGINAL, Glass	2 00
URINOMETER, in case	6 00

ATOMIZERS.

Every Atomizer is tested before being packed.

In case of the atomizer flow being stopped: 1. See that the points are not bent. 2. With the mouth blow water through the tubes. 3. Dissolve any gum that may be collected in the tube for fluid by alcohol. 4. Or pass a fine wire cleaner through the tubes, being careful not to injure the atomizing hole.

IMPROVED PHENIX THROAT ATOMIZER.

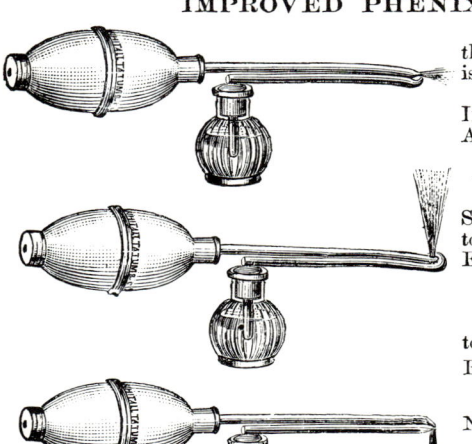

This Atomizer has a long tube adapted to reaching the diseased part of the throat by direct application. It is applied with one hand, leaving the other free.

	Per Doz.
IMPROVED, each in box	$6 00
ALL GLASS	8 00

ATOMIZER FOR NASAL CAVITIES.

For Catarrh and diseases of Nasal Cavities. The Spray issues from the Atomizer *upward* at a right angle to the tube.

Each in box . . . . Per Doz. 6 00

ATOMIZER FOR LARYNX.

The Spray is blown straight downward at a right angle to the tube.

Each in box . . . . Per Doz. 6 00

DELANO ATOMIZER.

No. 558, for the Throat 13 00

IMPERIAL ATOMIZER.

A new style with CORRUGATED BULB, TOP VALVE, and RELIABLE FITTINGS. A CAP accompanies each, so that the bottle can also be used as a Sprinkler. A WIRE CLEANER is in each box.

Per Doz.
IMPERIAL ATOMIZER, No. 828, Heavy 2 oz. Lubin, handsomely engraved 4 50

PHENIX ATOMIZER

The low price of this Atomizer, $1.50 per dozen, allows the Druggist to place it on his stand filled with Cologne at a less cost than the usual 25 ct. Colognes.

In neat boxes of **1** dozen each, with a WIRE CLEANER for each Atomizer.

Per Gross.
437. S. 1 oz. BELL STYLE (7½ drachms) $18 00
823. 1 oz. BRILLIANT, (see cut page 21) . 18 00
861. S. 1 oz. LUBIN (Takes Lettered Plate) 7½ drachms, (see cut page 22) 18 00
889. CONE, 3 panels (Takes Lettered Plate) 18 00

437. Bell Style.

Imperial Atomizer, No. 828.

We can for $2.00, the price of engraving, insert any design on 861 or 889, and furnish one gross or more of Atomizers at the regular price. We can accommodate these Atomizers to most of the small bottles on our Perfumery List.

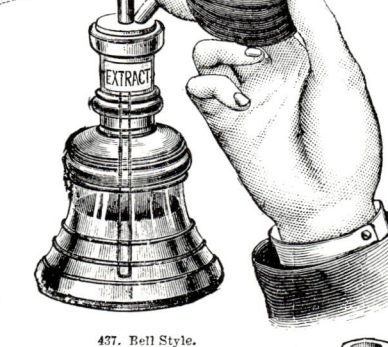
889. Cone, 3 Panel.

MISCELLANEOUS.
AT NET PRICES.

HYPODERMIC SYRINGES.

The metal work is finely nickel plated, the points are of best quality of steel, hardened and tempered. They are warranted not to leak.

	Per Doz
No. 1. With Glass Barrel, Nickel Plated Caps, graduated on the Glass	$15 00
No. 2. Same as No. 1, but graduated on the Piston Rod	15 00
No. 3. With Graduated Glass Barrel, protected by a fenestrated metal cylinder	21 00
Same, with Platinum Points	24 00
No. 5. With Metal Barrel, Nickel Plated, no glass, least liable to accidents of any in market; graduated on the Piston Rod,	18 00

The above are put up each in a neat morocco case, with vials, two points of different sizes.

No. 10. Extra size, Fenestrated, with three Platinum Points and double bearing for fingers 48 00

FEVER THERMOMETERS.

Indestructible Scale. Self-Registering.
Scale engraved on Tube.
¼ degree.

	Per Doz.
No. 275. Safety Contraction	24 00
No. 276. 4, 5 and 6 inch	20 00
No. 300. Lens shape, for magnifying the scale	28 00
No. 310. Siphon	30 00

Each Thermometer is packed in handsome hard rubber case.

TOOTHACHE DROPPER.
GLASS, WITH RUBBER BULB.

The bulb draws up just enough Toothache liquid to fill the reservoir. A cork cup then secures the contents, and it is ready for application immediately in the tooth by a gentle pressure in the bulb. Recommended by Dentists and Apothecaries.

Per Doz.
On cards of one dozen $1 50
To be filled by the Druggist and retailed at 25 cts.

BOUGIES AND CATHETERS.

BOUGIES.

	Per Doz.
English, ordinary. Numbers 1 to 12	1 12
English, Olive Point. Numbers 1 to 12	3 50

CATHETERS.

English, ordinary. Numbers 1 to 12	1 25
English, Olive Point. Numbers 1 to 12	4 00

SCALE OF DIAMETERS FOR BOUGIES AND CATHETERS.

PATENT WOOD-LINED PAPER BOXES.

These boxes are considered an improvement on the *Veneer Boxes*, and are sold at less than one-half their price.

They are stronger.
They resist the action of grease better.
They are not liable to warp and separate.

Per Gross.
¼ ounce, 1¼ inch diameter, ⅞ inch high . . 1 40
½ ounce, 1¾ inch diameter, 1 inch high . . 1 50
1 ounce, 2 inch diameter, 1¼ inch high . . 1 70
2 ounce, 2 inch diameter, 1⅝ inch high . . 2 50

Put up in papers of 3 doz. either size; or Assorted, 1 dozen each of 3 smaller sizes, per package 45 cts.

Paper Boxes of All Styles.

DRAWER PULLS.

SECTION 1.

SECTION 2.

COMPLETE.

We can furnish our improved DRAWER PULLS in Bronze or Nickel Plate.

The cut shows the Pull complete. Section 1 is the face of the Pull, which is fastened to the drawer by two screws (one at each end.) Then the label is laid on Section 2, and it is pushed up under Section 1 until the screw-holes at top of both are opposite, when it is fastened by a screw going through both plates, so that the label can be removed and changed by taking out the top screw, and without removing the face of the Pull from the drawer. This arrangement gives the Pull a solid iron back, so that the glass label is protected, and also gives a much larger space for the hand to take hold of than that found in any other Pull. The prices for Drawer Pulls are net.

PRICES OF IMPROVED DRAWER PULLS.

Per Doz.
Large Bronze, 5 in. by $2\frac{1}{4}$ inches $3 00
Small Bronze, $4\frac{1}{4}$ in. by 2 inches 2 85
Large Nickel Plated, 5 inch by $2\frac{1}{4}$ inch . . 4 00
Small Nickel Plated, $4\frac{1}{4}$ inch by 2 inch . . 3 50

Above prices are for Pulls complete, with screws, and Glass Labels lettered to order.

PRICES OF IMPROVED DRAWER PULLS.
Without Labels.

Per Doz.
Large Bronze, without Labels $2 25
Small Bronze, without Labels 2 10
Large Nickel Plated, without Labels 3 25
Small Nickel Plated, without Labels 2 75

PORCELAIN DRAWER PULLS.
WITH BLACK LETTERS.

Per Doz.
Large Plain Oval $2 50
Small Plain Oval 2 50

BRACKETS FOR SHOW BOTTLES.

Per Doz.
No. 3. 6 inch Bronze $13 50
No. 3. 7 inch Bronze 16 00
No. 4. 6 inch Bronze 12 00
No. 4. 7 inch Bronze 13 50

SPRINKLERS AND POWDER TUBES.

No. 100.

No. 4, Slip Cap.

No. 21.

COMPLETE, WITH CORKS.

Per Gross.
No. 100. Screw Cap, Nickel Plated $3 25
No. 4. Slip Cap 3 25
No. 4. Screw Cap 3 75
No. 21. Screw Cap. To screw on bottle . . 3 00
Large Acorn Cap for Wide Mouth Tooth Powders, $6.50.

No. 21. Acorn Screw Cap. Per Gross.
To screw on bottle . . $3 50

The above are for Liquids or Powders.

21. C R Valve. To screw on bottle . . 3 25
C R Valve. Shell cork . . . 3 50
This style is for liquids and acts by loosening the top without taking it off. When screwed tight the Valve seals the bottle perfectly. It is adjusted so that it cannot be lost.

See Nos. 645, 646, 902 and 903.

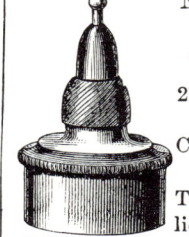

21 C. R. Acorn Cap, full size.

C. R. Shell Cork.

MISCELLANEOUS.

TOOTH POWDERS.

WIDE MOUTH, ROUND.
WITH ACORN TOPS.

	Per Doz.
1½ oz.	90
3 oz.	95

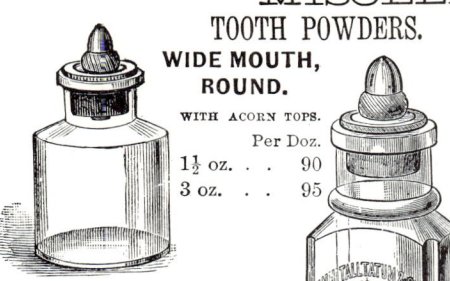

WIDE MOUTH—OBLONG.

	Per Doz.
1½ oz.	1 00
3 oz.	1 10

SHORT ROUND.

	Per Doz.
1½ oz.	65
3 oz.	70

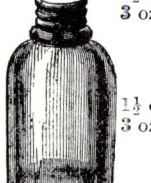
Short Round.

TALL ROUND.

	Per Doz.
2 oz.	65

FLUTED, ACORN TOP.

	Per Doz.
1½ oz.	70
3 oz.	75

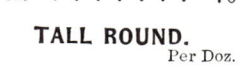
Tall Round.

ROUNDED CONE.

	Per Doz.
1½ oz.	70
3 oz.	75

For wide Mouth Tooth Powder Bottles, see also Nos. 605, 606 and 614.

Fluted—Acorn Top.

SPRINKLE TOP BOTTLES.
LUBIN.

	Per Doz.
¾ oz.	60
1 oz.	65

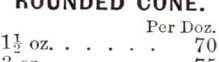
Rounded Cone.

NEW COLOGNE.

	Per Doz.
1 oz.	70
2 oz.	75
4 oz.	85
8 oz.	1 15
16 oz.	1 65

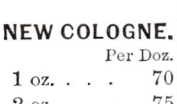
Lubin.

For the above with Chromo labels, see page 69.

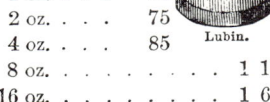
New Cologne.

OINTMENT POTS.
PATCH BOXES WITH GLASS COVERS.
ASSORTED COLORS.
Flint, Amber, Blue or Dk. Green.

	Per Doz.
½ oz.	70
1 oz.	75
2 oz.	90
4 oz.	1 05
8 oz.	1 30
16 oz.	1 65
1½ oz. (Inside Flange to Lid)	75

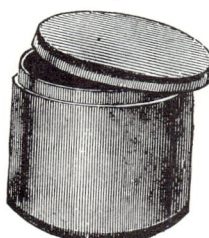

SHORT STYLE.
Flint, Amber, Blue or Dark Green.
Per Dozen.

	Caps of	Fancy Metal.	White Metal.	French Jet.
¼ oz.		40	50	50
½ oz.		45	55	55
1 oz.		55	65	65
2 oz.		65	75	75
4 oz.		85	1 00	

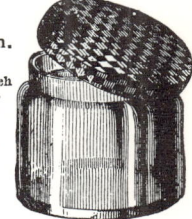

TALL STYLE or GALLIPOTS.
OPAL GLASS.
Per Dozen.

	Caps of	Fancy Metal.	White Metal.	French Jet.
¼ oz.		50	60	60
½ oz.		55	65	65
1 oz.		65	75	75
2 oz.		75	85	85
3 oz.		90	1 00	
4 oz.		1 00	1 10	

OPAL BOXES.
Per Doz.

½ oz. Opal Boxes, Opal Covers	80
1 oz. Opal Boxes, Opal Covers	90
2 oz. Opal Boxes, Opal Covers	1 00

COLD CREAM.
Opal with Sunk Letters in Red.
A new and very neat style.

	Per Doz.
½ oz. COLD CREAM,	90
1 oz. COLD CREAM,	1 00
½ oz. Unlettered,	80
1 oz. Unlettered,	90

Earthenware—Burnt Labels.

	Per Doz.
½ oz. COLD CREAM	90
1 oz. COLD CREAM	1 00
2 oz. COLD CREAM	1 10

OBLONG OPAL BOX.

	Per Doz.
¾ oz.	1 10

Oblong Opal Box.

POMADE JAR.
GLASS TOP GROUND ON.
FLINT GLASS.

	Per Doz.
4 oz.	1 20

PHENIX GRADUATES.

LINES AND NUMBERS CONSPICUOUSLY ENGRAVED ACCORDING TO THE AMERICAN STANDARD OF GRADUATION.

The American Dispensatory, the American Pharmaceutical Association, and the General Government, have all adopted as the standard of use and of law, 455.6 *Troy Grains of Water at 60° F as equal 1 fluid oz.*

So many Foreign Graduates, and Graduates made by Foreign Standards, have been in use, that much conflict with the standard of American dispensing has occurred. We have therefore prepared a Series Graduated by weight, with the utmost care, upon the American Standard. The Graduating is done directly from the weighed water, and not by afterwards engraving from the marks made on the side of the glass. Thus a constant source of error is avoided. *Each graduation is re-examined after it is cut, before the weighed water is emptied out.* We therefore feel confidence in guaranteeing the accuracy of the Phenix Series of Graduates.

THE GRADUATES ARE ALL DOUBLE SCALE.

Cone Shape.

	Per Doz.
½ oz.	$3 00
1 oz.	3 00
2 oz.	4 00
3 oz.	4 75
4 oz.	5 50
6 oz.	7 00
8 oz.	8 00
12 oz.	10 00
16 oz.	12 00
32 oz.	21 00

Cylindrical on Foot 25 per cent. extra. Stoppered 25 cents net each extra.

MINIM GRADUATES.

The 1 and 2 drachms have a very heavy base and cannot easily be overturned.

	Per Doz.
1 drachm or 60 minims	$4 00
2 drachms or 120 minims	4 50
MATCHLESS, Cone shape, Graduated, up to 1 ounce	8 00

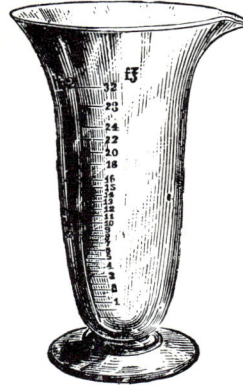

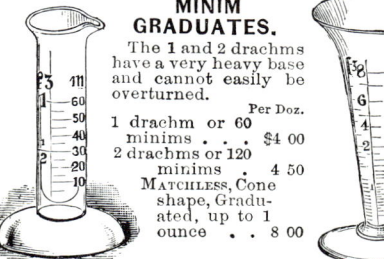

Matchless.

MEDICINE GLASSES, ENGRAVED.

No. 1. COMBINATION. Graduated on three sides with Minims, Tablespoon and Teaspoon marks,	$5 00
No. 2. S. Tumbler, T. & T. punted	2 75
No. 3. L. Tumbler, T. & T. punted	3 00
No. 4. Goblet, T. &T. punted	2 75
No. 5. Castor Oil, T. & T. punted	4 00

No. 5. No. 4.

PRESSED MEDICINE TUMBLERS.

	Per Doz.
S. Tea and Table Spoon	$1 25
L. Tea and Table Spoon	1 50
Tea and Table Spoon, Goblet Shape	2 00

The Prescription Pipette

is a substitute for the Graduate, being *more exact, requiring less time, and saving the soiling of the Shelf Bottles.*

	Each.
8 drachms and minims	$1 00
4 drachms and minims	80

GRAM GRADUATES.

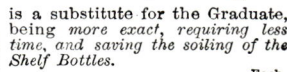

Cylindrical on Foot.

	Cone Shape.		Cylindrical on foot.
	Per Doz.		Each.
30 grams,	30 CC	$4 50	60
50 grams,	50 CC	5 25	70
100 grams,	100 CC	6 75	1 00
200 grams,	200 CC	7 50	1 50
250 grams,	250 CC	8 25	2 00
500 grams,	500 CC	15 75	2 50
1,000 grams,	1,000 CC	27 00	3 00

GRADUATED FLASKS

	Per Dozen.	
	For Corks.	Stoppered.
50 CC	6 00	9 00
100 CC	7 00	10 00
¼ Liter,	8 00	11 00
½ Liter,	12 00	15 00
1 Liter,	21 00	24 00
2 Liter,	27 00	30 00

DOUBLE GRADUATES.

ENGLISH MEASURE ON ONE SIDE & METRIC MEASURE ON THE OTHER. CONE SHAPE.

	Per Doz.
1 drachm or 60 minims, and 4 grams,	$6 00
1 ounce and 30 grams,	5 25
2 ounce and 50 grams,	6 00
3 ounce and 75 grams,	7 25
4 ounce and 100 grams,	8 00
8 ounce and 200 grams,	9 00
8 ounce and 250 grams,	9 75
12 ounce and 300 grams,	11 25
16 ounce and 400 grams,	15 50
16 ounce and 500 grams,	18 75
32 ounce and 1,000 grams,	32 25

GRADUATED PERCOLATING JARS.

For Receiving the Percolate.

			Per Doz
Quarts,	$12 50	1 Gallon,	$31 00
½ Gallon,	19 00	2 Gallon,	42 00

GRADUATES.

Vom Hofe's Patent Ring Graduates.

The lines on the Patent Ring graduates (which are engraved) go all around the glass, so that a level can be obtained without difficulty, thus insuring greater accuracy in measuring.

The graduations are made by standard of avoirdupois weight, with Distilled Water at 60° F., so that the 16 oz. mark indicates the bulk of water weighing 1 ℔. avoirdupois.

The greatest care is taken to insure correctness in every respect, so that we feel assured in placing them before our customers that they will meet with the confidence deserved by careful workmanship and the greatest obtainable accuracy.

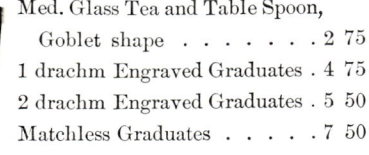

	Per Doz.
½ oz.	$3 00
1 oz.	3 00
2 oz.	4 00
3 oz.	4 75
4 oz.	5 50
6 oz.	7 00
8 oz.	8 00
12 oz.	10 00
16 oz.	12 00
32 oz.	21 00
Med. Glass Tea and Table Spoon, Tumbler shape	2 75
Med. Glass Tea and Table Spoon, Goblet shape	2 75
1 drachm Engraved Graduates	4 75
2 drachm Engraved Graduates	5 50
Matchless Graduates	7 50

GRAM GRADUATES.
(Cubic Centimeters.)
CONE SHAPE, PATENT RING.

		Per Doz.
30 grams,	30 C. C.	$4 50
50 grams,	50 C. C.	5 25
75 grams,	75 C. C.	6 00
100 grams,	100 C. C.	6 75
200 grams,	200 C. C.	7 50
250 grams,	250 C. C.	8 25
300 grams,	300 C. C.	9 00
400 grams,	400 C. C.	12 75
500 grams,	500 C. C.	15 75
1,000 grams,	1,000 C. C.	27 00

CYLINDRICAL ON FOOT.

		Each.
10 grams,	10 C. C.	$ 50
50 grams,	50 C. C.	70
100 grams,	100 C. C.	1 00
200 grams,	200 C. C.	1 50
250 grams,	250 C. C.	2 00
500 grams,	500 C. C.	2 50
1,000 grams,	1,000 C. C.	3 00

Our Gram Graduates are made especially for us, and we warrant them to be correct.

ENGRAVED GRADUATES.
ENGLISH MEASURE ON ONE SIDE AND METRICAL MEASURE ON THE OTHER.

Cone Shape.

		Per Doz.
1 drachm or 60 drops, and 4 grams,		$6 00
1 ounce and	30 grams,	5 25
2 ounce and	50 grams,	6 00
3 ounce and	75 grams,	7 25
4 ounce and	100 grams,	8 00
8 ounce and	200 grams,	9 00
8 ounce and	250 grams,	9 75
12 ounce and	300 grams,	11 25
16 ounce and	400 grams,	15 50
16 ounce and	500 grams,	18 75
32 ounce and	1,000 grams,	32 25

OINTMENT JARS.

GLASS, FLAT TOP.

Flint, Dark Green, Blue, Amber, and Opal.

	Per Doz.
½ oz.	$ 70
1 oz.	75
2 oz.	90
4 oz.	1 05
8 oz.	1 30
16 oz.	1 65

WHITE, FLAT TOP.

	Per Doz.
¼ pound	$1 05
½ pound	1 30
1 pound	1 55
1½ pound	2 25
2 pound	2 60
3 pound	3 90
4 pound	6 50

WHITE, STEEPLE TOP.

	Per Doz.
¼ pound	$1 80
½ pound	2 10
1 pound	2 30
1½ pound	3 60
2 pound	4 80
3 pound	6 00
4 pound	9 00
6 pound	11 70

BLUE, STEEPLE TOP.

	Per Doz.
¼ pound	$2 70
½ pound	3 00
1 pound	3 30
1½ pound	4 80
2 pound	6 00
3 pound	9 00
4 pound	10 80
6 pound	14 40

WHITE, STEEPLE TOP, GILT BAND.

	Per Doz.
½ pound	$4 50
1 pound	5 40
1½ pound	7 20
2 pound	9 00

PORCELAIN PATCH BOXES.

	Per Gross.
¼ oz.	$9 00
½ oz.	9 00
¾ oz.	10 50
1 oz.	10 50
1½ oz.	12 00
2 oz.	12 50
3 oz.	15 00
4 oz.	18 00

PORCELAIN LEECH JARS.

	Each.
Quart	$4 50
½ Gallon	5 00
Gallon	5 50
2 Gallon	6 00

EVAPORATING DISHES.

BERLIN PORCELAIN.

No.		Per Doz.
00.	2 oz.	$3 50
0.	4 oz.	4 50
1.	8 oz.	5 50
2.	Pint	7 80
3.	Quart	10 00
4.	3 Pint	12 00
5.	½ Gallon	15 60
6.	¾ Gallon	21 00
7.	1 Gallon	27 00
8.	1¼ Gallon	33 00
9.	1½ Gallon	39 00
10.	1¾ Gallon	48 00
11.	2½ Gallon	54 00
12.	3 Gallon	60 00

GERMAN PORCELAIN.

Glazed inside, with Heavy Rim around the top.

No.	Diameter.	Content.	Each.
00.	16 inch,	3 Gallon	$5 00
0.	15 inch,	2 Gallon	3 50
1.	13 inch,	1 Gallon	2 10
2.	12 inch,	3 Quarts	1 75
3.	11 inch,	½ Gallon	1 30
4.	10 inch,	3 Pints	1 00
5.	9 inch,	Quart	85
6.	8 inch,	24 oz.	75
7.	7 inch,	20 oz.	65
8.	6 inch,	16 oz.	65
9.	5½ inch,	8 oz.	45

SUNDRIES.

WEDGWOOD FUNNELS.
RIBBED INSIDE.

		Per Doz.
No. 1	3 inch diameter	$3 50
No. 2	4 inch diameter	4 00
No. 3	5 inch diameter	5 50
No. 4	6 inch diameter	8 00
No. 5	7 inch diameter	12 50
No. 6	7½ inch diameter	16 50
No. 7	8 inch diameter	21 00
No. 8	9 inch diameter	24 00
No. 9	10 inch diameter	30 00
No. 10	11 inch diameter	36 00

For Glass Funnels, see page 38.

PILL TILES.
GRADUATED.

	Per Doz.
5 inch	$4 50
6 inch	6 00
8 inch	9 00
10 inch	13 50
12 inch	24 00
6 x 8 inch	9 00
8 x 10 inch	13 50
10 x 12 inch	24 00

MORTARS AND PESTLES.
GLASS.

	Per Doz.
1 oz.	2 40
2 oz.	2 40
3 oz.	3 00
4 oz.	3 00
8 oz.	4 80
16 oz.	6 00
32 oz.	9 00

WEDGWOOD.

		Per Doz.
0000—	3 inches across top	4 32
000—	3¼ inches across top	5 04
00—	3½ inches across top	6 00
0—	4 inches across top	6 72
1—	4½ inches across top	7 80
2—	5 inches across top	10 20
3—	6 inches across top	12 00
4—	6½ inches across top	15 00
5—	7 inches across top	19 50
6—	8 inches across top	24 00
7—	8½ inches across top	30 00
8—	9½ inches across top	39 00
9—10½	inches across top	48 00
10—12	inches across top	54 00
11—13	inches across top	63 00
12—14	inches across top	72 00

BED PANS.
EARTHENWARE.

	Per Doz.
No. 1—White	$9 00
No. 1—Yellow	7 80

URINALS.

	Per Doz.
Male, White Earthenware	7 20
Female, White Earthenware	7 20
Male, Glass	4 50
Female, Glass	4 50

SPATULAS.

Steel—Patent Cocoa Handles—Riveted.

	Per Doz.
3 inch	2 50
4 inch	2 85
5 inch	3 35
6 inch	4 00
7 inch	5 10
8 inch	6 25
9 inch	8 40
10 inch	10 45
11 inch	14 00
12 inch	18 50

Steel—Patent Ebony Handles—With Nickel Tips and Bolsters.

	Per Doz.
3 inch	3 55
4 inch	3 90
5 inch	4 30
6 inch	5 00
7 inch	5 75
8 inch	7 00
9 inch	9 25
10 inch	12 80
11 inch	17 10
12 inch	21 40

CORKS.

TAPER VIAL.
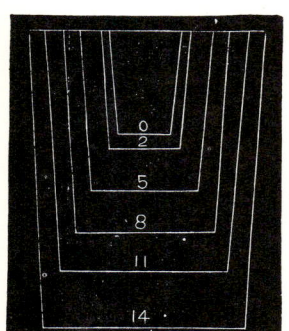

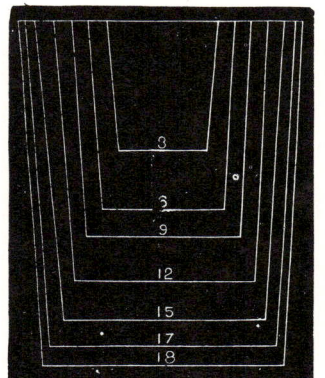

TAPER VIAL.
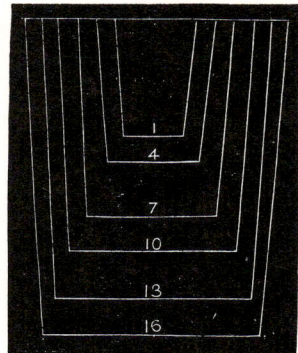

TAPER VIAL CORKS.

	Per Gross.		
	Superfine,	Fine.	Common.
No. 1, ... $	cents.	cents.
No. 2, ...	do.	do.
No. 3, ...	do.	do.
No. 4, ...	do.	do.
No. 5, ...	do.	do.
No. 6, ...	do.	do.
No. 7, ...	do.	do.
No. 8, ...	do.	do.
No. 9, ...	do.	do.
No. 10, ...	do.	do.
No. 11, ...	do.	do.
No. 12, ...	do.	do.
1 to 6, assorted, . , . . .	do.	
3 to 8, assorted, ...	do.	

Also, Homeopathic Vial Corks.

RUBBER CORKS. Per 100.

No. 1, ... $	
No. 2, ...	
No. 2½, ...	
No. 3, ...	
No. 4, ...	
No. 4½, ...	
No. 5, ...	
No. 5½, ...	
No. 6, ...	
No. 6½, ...	
No. 7, ...	

FLAT JAR CORKS.

	Per Gross.	
	Superfine.	Fine.
1 inch diameter, ... $	$
1⅛ inch do.		
1¼ inch do.		
1⅜ inch do.		
1½ inch do.		
1⅝ inch do.		
1¾ inch do.		
1⅞ inch do.		
2 inch do.		
2⅛ inch do.		
2¼ inch do.		
2⅜ inch do.		
2½ inch do.		
2⅝ inch do.		
2¾ inch do.		
2⅞ inch do.		
3 inch do.		
3¼ inch do.		
3½ inch do.		
3¾ inch do.		

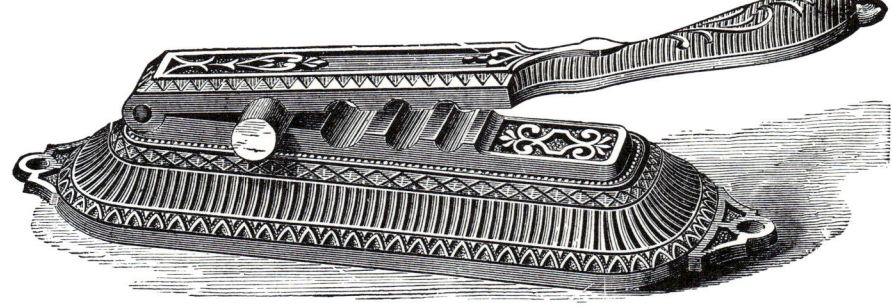

CORK PRESSES.

		Per Doz.
No. 0.	Japanned, ...	$3 00
No. 1.	Dark Bronze, ...	4 80
No. 2.	Verde Antique, ...	6 00

MISCELLANEOUS.

COMBINED STOPPER AND DROPPER.

This cut represents the new Stopper and Dropper combined in one piece made of rubber. It consists of a double Coned Stopper—one End Grooved on opposite sides to admit air and permit liquids to drop regularly; the other End acts as a tight Stopper, to be reversed as needed.

The advantage of this over all others in the market is its Cheapness, Utility, and being so easily cleansed.

In boxes of 25 Large, and 25 Small.

	Per Box.
1 to 6 oz	$1.00

PILL MACHINES.

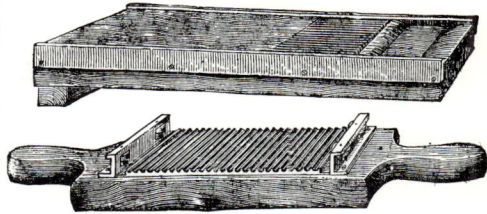

With Brass Plates and Brass Sides, and Walnut Rolling Board.

Each machine warranted to turn out perfectly round Pills, and the full number of grooves at every operation. The sides of the Rolling Board are of the requisite height to roll the stick just the size of the groove and pill, thereby insuring a perfect pill.

These machines, as now constructed, will turn out more pills in any given time, than any other in the market.

PRICES.

				Each.
12 Pills, 3 gr., 4 gr., 5 gr., either size				$3 50
18 " 3 " 4 " 5 " " "				4 50
24 " 3 " 4 " 5 " " "				5 50

Side Rollers, $1 extra.

Machines for 30, 36, 50 Pills. Any size made to order. Also,

Pill Machines for making Compressed Pills.

CORK SCREWS.

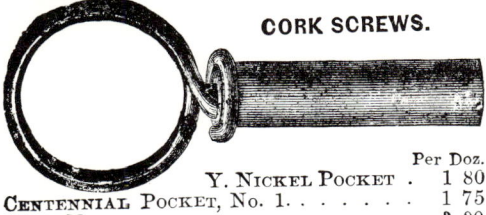

	Per Doz.
Y. Nickel Pocket	1 80
Centennial Pocket, No. 1	1 75
Acme Nickel	3 30
Acme Power Nickel	3 67

A.   B.   C.

C. Extra.

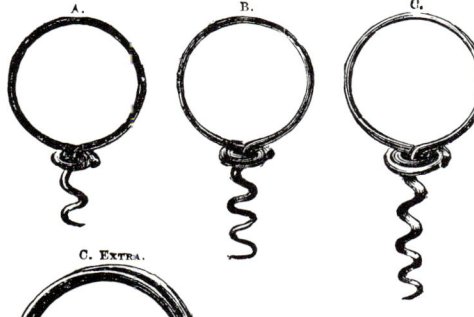

WIRE CORK RINGS.

	Per Gross.
A. 1 doz. in Box, 12 Boxes in Carton	1 00
B. " "	1 25
C. " "	1 50
C. Extra	2 00
A. B. and C. Assorted, 1 doz. in Box, 12 boxes in Carton	1 25
A. In 1 Gross Boxes	50
B. " "	65
C. " "	80
C. Extra " "	1 00

PATENT FILTER RACK AND DREG SQUEEZER COMBINED.

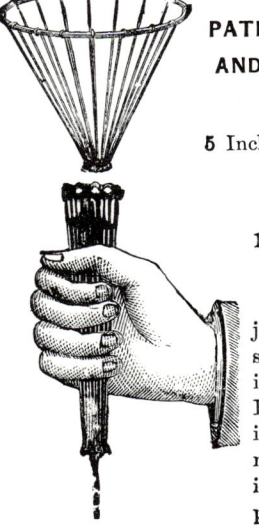

	Per Doz.
5 Inch	$3 75
7 Inch	5 00
9 "	7 00
12 "	8 00

This Rack can be adjusted to any smaller size by simply unfastening the joint on the Rubber hoop and coiling to the desired diameter. The Funnel can in most cases be dispensed with.

To squeeze out the Dregs left on the paper after filtering, it will be found most valuable, and by employing it on expensive Drugs, enough is saved, in *only once using*, to pay the cost of the Squeezer.

When hung on two nails, it will form a semicircular Wall Pocket, handy as a Twineholder, etc. Suspended on three cords it makes a useful Hanging Basket.

STOPPERED COLOGNES.
AT NET PRICES.

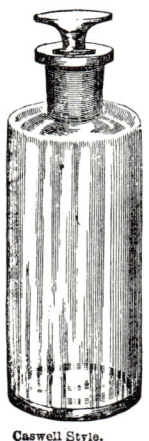

881.   581.   882.   Caswell Style.   890.

We call attention to these lines of Cut and Engraved Ware of our own manufacture. They include entirely new styles for the 1879-1880 season. Samples sent at dozen price on application.

	Per Dozen.
823. 1 oz. ROUND BRILLIANT	$1 40
824. 2 oz. ROUND BRILLIANT	1 50
859 A. 1 oz. FLUTED OCTAGON, Hollow Ball Stopper, Cut (Plain see p. 22)	2 00
860 A. 2 oz. FLUTED OCTAGON, Hollow Ball Stopper, Cut (Plain see p. 22)	2 20
880. 4 oz. FLUTED OCTAGON, Hollow Ball Stopper, (Imitation Cut)	1 80
880 A. 4 oz. FLUTED OCTAGON, Hexagon Stopper, Cut and Engraved (Plain see p. 23)	3 80
864 A. 1 oz. ROUND, very heavy, Hollow Globe Stopper, Eng'd (Plain see p. 23)	1 50
865 A. 2 oz. ROUND, very heavy, Hollow Globe Stopper, Eng'd (Plain see p. 23)	1 90
881 A. 2 oz. CONE, Cut (Plain see p. 23)	5 00
890 A. 2 oz. OVAL BRILLIANT, Cut (Plain see p. 23)	5 00
882 A. S. ½ Pint THATCHED CONE, Cut Lapidary Stopper (Plain see p. 23)	4 20
882 B. S ½ Pint THATCHED CONE, Cut Lapidary Stopper, and engraved	5 00
539 A. S. ½ Pint Round BURNETT, engraved, (Plain see p. 24)	2 00
Pint Round BURNETT (see p. 24)	
541. A. ½ Pint CASWELL, Engraved, (Plain see p. 24)	2 60
543. A. Pint CASWELL, Engraved, (Plain see p. 24)	3 50
553. L. ½ Pint POMEGRANATE, Pear Stopper, cut on top (see p. 24)	
554. L. ½ Pt. DIAMOND BRILLIANT, Diamond Stopper (see p. 24)	
557 A. Tall R. S. ½ Pt. "COLOGNE." Cut Wreath, Hollow Cut Stopper (Plain see p. 24)	5 00

	Per Dozen.
558 A. Same "COLOGNE." Cut Grapes and Bird. Hollow Cut St. (Plain see p. 24)	6 50
FOR COVERING WITH SILK.	
559 A. Tall ½ Pint, S. F. STYLE, FLAT HOLLOW Cut Stopper. As USED FOR COVERING WITH SILK	2 50
B. Same, with Cut LAPIDARY Stopper	2 50
560 A. Tall Pint S. F. STYLE, FLAT HOLLOW Cut Stopper	3 00
B. Same, Cut LAPIDARY Stopper	3 00
561 A. Tall Qt. S. F. STYLE, FLAT HOLLOW Cut Stopper	4 50
B. Same, Cut LAPIDARY Stopper	4 50

559, 560, 561.

IRON MOULD BOTTLES or TINCTURES, with CUT STOPPERS, LAPIDARY or FLAT HOLLOW, are serviceable at a less cost. The bottles being covered the difference in the glass does not appear.

IRON MOULD TINCTURE WITH CUT STOPPER.

Short ¼ Pint (574)	1 75
½ Pints	2 00
Pints	2 50
Quarts	3 50
564 A. ¼ Pint EGG SHAPE, Engraved and Cut, Pear Stopper (Plain see p. 24)	5 25
565 A. ½ Pint EGG SHAPE, Engraved and Cut, Pear Stopper (Plain see p. 24)	7 00
566 A. 5 oz. HEAVY SQUARE, Engraved, and Cut Lapidary Stopper (Plain see p. 24)	4 00
567 A. 10 oz. HEAVY SQUARE, Engraved and Cut Lapidary Stopper (Plain see p. 24)	6 00

COLOGNES.

STOPPERED COLOGNES.—At Net Prices.

556.

562, 563.

555.

570, 572, Sachet.

	Per Doz.
555. L. ½ Pint FLUTED BASE AND SHOULDER, Fancy Stopper (see p. 24) .	
555 A. L. ½ Pint FLUTED BASE AND SHOULDER, Engraved Wreath	$4 50
555 B. L. ½ Pint FLUTED BASE AND SHOULDER, Engraved, Grape Pattern .	5 00
¼ Pint DIAMOND (see p. 24)	
556 A. ¼ Pint DIAMOND, cut	8 00
556 B. ¼ Pint DIAMOND, extra cut . . .	12 00
562 A. 5 oz. CONE, Cut Neck, 3 Wreath Pattern, Cut Lapidary Stopper . .	5 00
563 A. 10 oz. CONE, Cut Neck, 3 Wreath Pattern, Cut Lapidary Stopper . .	7 50

	Per Doz.
570. ½ Pint SACHET, Cut Stopper	6 50
570 A. ½ Pint SACHET, Finely Eng'd Wreath and Name, Cut Stopper	9 00
571. Pint SACHET, Cut Stopper	9 50
571 A. Pt. SACHET, Eng'd W'th & Name, C. St.	13 00
572. Quart SACHET, Cut Stopper	15 00
572 A. Quart SACHET, Engr'd Wreath and Name, Cut Stopper	20 00
¼ Pint SHORT COLOGNE (see p. 24). .	
575 A. ½ Pint OCTAGON FLUTED "COLOGNE."	
½ Pint OCT. MONUMENT (see p. 24) .	
581 A. ½ Pint DIAMOND GLOBE, Fancy St. .	

GLASS LABELED CHROMO COLOGNES.

	Per Doz
¼ Pint CASWELL STYLE, with Glass Chromo Label	2 75
½ Pint CASWELL STYLE, with Glass Chromo Label	3 25
Pint CASWELL STYLE, with Glass Chromo Label	3 75
½ Pint CASWELL STYLE, { Oval Recess } with Glass Chromo Label . .	3 25
Pint CASWELL STYLE, { Shield Recess } with Glass Chromo Label . .	3 75

NEW STYLE SPRINKLE TOPS.

1 oz., with Glass Chromo Label (548 see page 24.)					2 50
2 oz.,	ditto	ditto	(549	ditto	2 60
4 oz.,	ditto	ditto	(550	ditto	2 75
8 oz.,	ditto	ditto	(551	ditto	3 00
16 oz.,	ditto	ditto	(552	ditto	3 50

Above can be labeled with chromo label, either "Cologne" or "Bay Rum," or assorted names to order, at above prices.

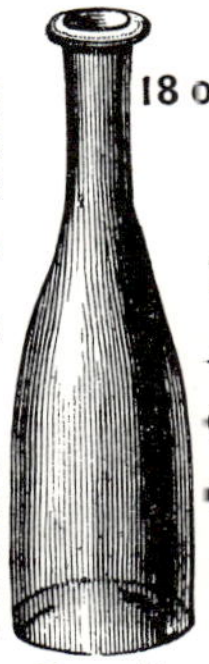

18 oz. Barbers' Bottle.

	Per Doz. For Corks.
Flint	1 25
Amber . . .	2 00
Opal Blue . .	2 00
Opal White .	2 00

(See also No. 882.)

GLASS LABELS.

For Shelf Bottles, Urns, Jars, Cologne Bottles, &c.

Estimates for fitting out stores with Glass Labels will be furnished on application. In asking for estimates, please state the shape, style, color, &c., of labels wanted; and the circumference of bottles used, if labels *only* are required.

For prices of Shelf Bottles, &c., see our List, pages 26 and 27.

Glass Cutting and Engraving done to order.

HENRY TROEMNER'S
FINE SCALES, BALANCES AND WEIGHTS, AT LOWEST PRICES.

Ebony Box Scale.

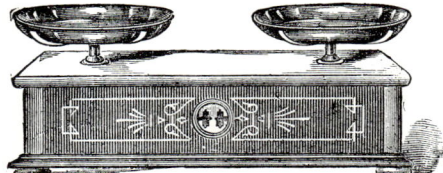

Ebony Box with Gold Lines and Dial Marble Top.

No.	Diam. of Pans.	Capacity.	Price.
0,	7 in.	10 lbs.	$14 00
1,	8 "	15 "	16 00
2,	9 "	25 "	19 00

"Queen Anne" Box Scales (New.)

Very Elegant Scale of the finest finish. Made "Queen Anne" Style. Box of Ebony and ornamented with gold lines. Has marble top and gilt dial.

No.	Diam. of Pans.	Capacity.	Price.
3,	9 in.	25 lbs.	$25 00

Prescription Scales. No. 13.

In Polished Mahogany Case. Counterpoised doors, sliding upward. Scale has 8¼ in. beam, 2¼ in. Nickel Pans, and is sensible to 1-50 grain. Being specially adapted to delicate weighing, such as poisons, etc., etc.

Price, ... $24 00

Prescription Scales. No. 36.

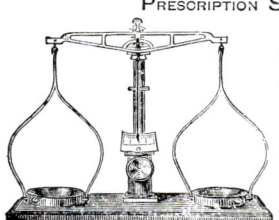

On Marble Base. With Lever, open beam. Highly finished. With weights.

No.	Pans.	Brass.	Nickel Plated.
1,	2½ in.	$9 00	$11 00
2,	2¾ "	10 50	12 50
3.	3 "	12 00	14 00

French Walnut Box Scale.

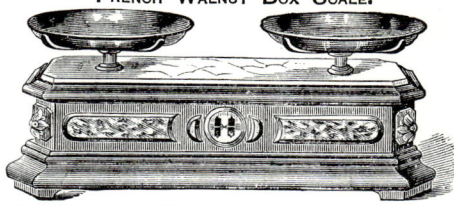

French Polished Walnut Box, richly ornamented with Carved Panels of Mottled Walnut, Marble Top, Gilt Dial.

No.	Diam. of Pans.	Capacity,	Price.
1,	9 in.	15 lbs.	$25 00
2,	10 "	25 "	28 00

Box Prescription Scale. No. 12.

French Polished Ebony Box, with Marble Top and hinged Glass Cover, countersunk Basin to keep the Weights in. Has 2¾ in. Nickel Plated Pans. Scale sensible to 1-30 grain.

Price $20 00
Extra large size, 3¾ in. Pans . 22 00

Army Prescription Scales.

On Mahogany Box. With weights.

No.	Beam.	Pans.	Price.
0,	8 in.	2¾ in.	$7 00
1,	7 "	2¼ "	5 50
2,	5½ "	2 "	4 00

"Agate" Prescription Scales. No. 88.

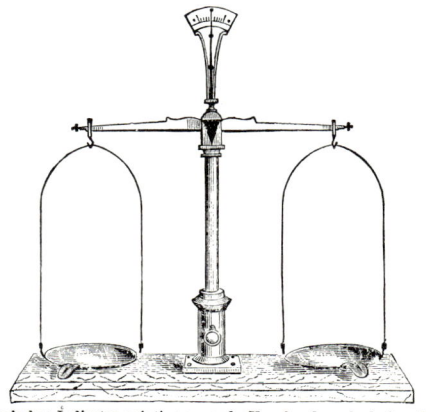

Scale has Indicator pointing upward. Very handsomely designed and finished. Beam heavily Plated with Gold. All other parts of the scale Nickel. Adjusting Screws on Beam by which the scale can always be quickly balanced. Marble Platform—ALL BEARINGS are of "Agate." Scale sensible to 1-100 grain.

No.	Beam.	Pans.	Price.
0,	9½ in.	3 in.	$26 00

A complete list will be sent upon application by mail.

WHITALL, TATUM AND COMPANY
an historical introduction

The history of glass manufacturing in America is as old as the country itself. As early as 1609, a glasshouse for the manufacture of bottles was established in the Jamestown colony. The glass it produced was the first manufactured article produced in the American colonies.

Early glassworks were likely, however, to be short-lived. The Jamestown enterprise, intended to supply domestic and foreign needs, failed in a short time, as did a subsequent glasshouse built in the colony in 1620. So did most pre-Revolutionary attempts to establish glassworks, due to a lack of skilled workmen, inability to compete with English imports, and the uncertainties of life in the new colonies.

One of the few successful early glasshouses was that founded by Caspar Wistar in 1739 at Wistarberg near Allowaystown in southern New Jersey. Conditions in that area were excellent for glassmaking. Sand, the basic raw material needed, was in abundant supply and of excellent quality, as was wood for fuel. A network of small creeks and rivers, feeding into the Delaware River, provided ready transportation to both domestic and foreign markets.

The Wistar works failed to survive the tumultuous economic conditions of the Revolutionary period and were closed in 1781. Other works, however, had been established at Glassboro in 1775. Founded by the Stanger brothers, former Wistar employees, this enterprise is the only Jersey glassworks that has operated continuously since the eighteenth century. Subsequently, it passed through the hands of several owners until its purchase by the Whitneys in 1837. As Whitney Brothers it produced a number of well-known historical flasks and bitters bottles. In 1918 it was purchased by the Owens Bottle Company.

In the decades immediately following the Revolution, American glassmaking flourished because of restrictive tariffs, and rising domestic need. Among the new glassworks started was a window-glass works at Port Elizabeth, New Jersey, founded by James Lee and a group of Philadelphia associates in 1801. Five years later they started another works, the parent firm of Whitall, Tatum to produce both window glass and bottles, at nearby Millville. In 1814 the works was purchased by Gideon Scull and production was converted to hollow ware.

The Millville firm passed through several hands, and, therefore, changes of name, in the early nineteenth century—Burgin and Wood (1829); Burgin, Wood and Pearsall (1830); Burgin and Pearsall (1833); Scattergood, Booth and Company (1836); Scattergood, Haverstick and Co. (1838); Scattergood and Whitall (1844); Whitall and Brothers (1845); and Whitall Brothers and Co. (1848).

John M. Whitall entered the business in 1838, and in 1845 I. F. Whitall joined his brother. In 1848 Edward Tatum entered the partnership. In the same year an office was opened in Philadelphia; a New York office was opened in 1852. In 1854 the firm acquired a second plant known as the Schetterville or South Millville works. This plant was—in time—to become the major facility of the company.

The South Millville plant had been founded in 1832 by two German glassblowers from Baltimore, Frederick and Phillip Schetter, as a window-glass works. The Schetters failed in business in 1844 and the plant was purchased by Lewis Mulford in association with William Coffin and A. K. Hay of the Hammonton Glass Works. Operated as Coffin, Mulford and Company, it was converted to a bottle house before being purchased by the Whitalls.

An 1891 view of the "Flint-Glass Factories" of Whitall, Tatum in South Millville.—
Illustration courtesy of Armstrong Cork Company

In 1857, when I. F. Whitall left the firm, the company gained a new name—Whitall, Tatum and Co. The company was incorporated as Whitall Tatum Company in 1901.

Manufacturing operations in both Millville and South Millville plants were carried out by small groups known as shops, each consisting of two to four men, with two or three boys to assist. Theoretically, therefore, glass manufacturing could be conducted as a small one-shop business, and small glasshouses proliferated in the south Jersey area. By 1869 there were 42 glasshouses in the state, of which ten were in Millville. Many of the smaller companies lasted for periods of only a few years.

Whitall, Tatum must have been well managed for it continued to grow and came to dominate glass production in Millville and, to some extent, on a national basis. By 1905 the two single largest bottle-producing centers in the United States were Muncie, Indiana, home of Ball Brothers, and Millville. Whitall, Tatum was responsible for the largest share of Millville's production.

During the later half of the nineteenth century finished products were shipped by rail *and* by water from the South Millville plant site on the Maurice River. The company itself owned at least five ships: two sloops, two schooners, and a steamboat.

The type of bottles produced by the company in the early years is not known. Presumably patent medicine bottles were a large part of the output, as they were for many early factories. Certainly by the time the 1880 catalog was issued, Whitall, Tatum seems to have been well established as a manufacturer and purveyor of medicine bottles, druggists' supplies and sundries, and laboratory glassware.

When James Lee founded the first glasshouse at Millville in 1806, many bottles were still completely handblown, as they had been for centuries. The work of the early glassmaker was that of an accomplished artisan.

A workman first gathered a glob of glass on the end of a hollow rod. He then smoothed it by rolling it over a flat metal plate or stone, meanwhile blowing into the rod to form a bubble in the molten glass. Finally, he shaped the bottle by swinging and swirling his blowpipe. Such handblown bottles were produced in fairly large quantities by Whitall, Tatum and other companies up until the Civil War and, for special purposes, for many years afterward.

An alternative method was that of blowing the bottle, still using human lungpower, into a two or three-part mold. This assured greater uniformity of size and shape and a decoration or the name of the bottle manufacturer or customer could be carved into the mold and would appear embossed on the bottle. The Whitall company employed a moldmaker as early as 1839 to turn out metal molds, and a department for this purpose was established at the South Millville plant in 1862.

One of the shops with a furnace installed in 1865. From the 1879 catalog.—*Illustration courtesy of Armstrong Cork Company*

The catalog issued in 1880 came during a time when the company was engaged in its most inventive and varied work. Groundwork for making an extensive line of wares had been laid in the years immediately following the Civil War. At that time a wooden mold shop, a department for manufacturing general laboratory glassware, and a lamp room for specialized ware were opened at South Millville. The production of lettered plate ware began in 1868. In 1870 the line was expanded with what was known as shop furniture, the large bottles in which druggists and chemists kept supplies.

A druggists' sundries department was opened in 1876, and the company also jobbed items made by others. The manufacture of perfumers' ware was begun in 1878. To produce the more elaborate models demanded by this market, engraving and cutting shops were opened.

The majority of ware produced at Whitall, Tatum, as the 1880 catalog displays, was strictly utilitarian. Run-of-the-mill bottles were indistinguishable from those made by the firm's competitors. Such shapes as Philadelphia Ovals, French Squares, and Union Ovals were produced by all. Unless a specimen is marked, it is impossible to tell whether it was made at Millville. It could just as well be the product of Hagerty Brothers and Co. of New York, or Fox, Fultz and Webster or Dean, Foster and Co., both of Boston.

The individuality of Whitall, Tatum's moldmakers, blowers and decorators is revealed, however, in some of the company's more elaborate wares. Poison bottles are one category in which each manufacturer displayed individual design. Made of brilliant cobalt glass to distinguish them by sight from ordinary bottles in the medicine chest, they were customarily blown into molds which produced a distinctive raised design on the surface of the bottle. It, then, could be recognized by touch in the dark. Two examples are shown in the 1880 catalog, both characterized by raised patterns of sharp diamond shapes.

A closer approach to glass as an art form was made in the design of perfumers' wares, colognes, barbers' bottles, and show jars. In these, deep cutting often brought out the brilliance of the material, or delicate engraving its fragility. Although these were purely commercial products, the Victorian fondness for elaborate adornment and solid workmanship is evident even in the line drawings used to illustrate the company's wares in the 1880 catalog.

As the century drew to a close, the show bottles, the showpieces of the Whitall, Tatum line, developed in variety and embellishment. Three and four-tiered confections displayed the fully-developed techniques of the glassmaker's art. Elaborate molds, colored glass, overlay, enameling, and gilding provided a richness of decoration that paralleled the contemporary production in brilliant cut glass and art glass. The exuberant curved shapes echo those to be found in much Victorian furniture.

A byproduct of this production was the offhand work for which Millville is perhaps most famous. It was the workers in Whitall, Tatum's wooden mold shop and the men who did the most delicate hand work in the lamp work room who, in their free time, turned out some of the best known of American paperweights. Among them was John Rhulander, creator of the molds for the pineapple show bottles. From 1863 to 1912, Rhulander and others produced many weights, including the Millville Rose, the Millville Lily, and the Jersey Devil.

Bottles made for special events or for particular customers are not, of course, shown in the 1880 catalog, or in other catalogs. Among these was an inkwell in the form of Independence Hall made for the Centennial of the American Revolution in 1876.

The success of Whitall, Tatum in the late nineteenth century and early years of the present century can be gauged by the opening of additional sales offices. By the 1890's distribution was both nationwide and international. To service customers a Boston office was added in 1898 to the existing sales facilities in New York and Philadelphia. By 1901 the company had a showroom in Chicago. In 1905 an office was opened in Sydney, Australia, and by 1916 there was one in Buenos Aires.

Since Whitall, Tatum was both a manufacturer of glass and a jobber of related wares, sold wholesale and retail, catalogs produced by the company were used in many ways. Each salesman and manager of the firm evidently had his own copy, specially bound in leather. The company, however, also sold through other distributors such as Bausch and Lomb.

Valued customers were institutions of higher learning such as those listed proudly on page 33 of the 1880 catalog. These organizations, as well as individual druggists and physicians, could order directly from the factory. Although this practice decreased as sales coverage improved, instructions in the catalogs indicate that a significant mail order business existed well into the twentieth century.

The advent of automatic bottling machinery presaged the end of the era in which each bottle, no matter how standard the shape, bore the stamp of a hand craft. Attempts at automation were instituted at Millville as early as 1899, and a partially automated machine for the production of wide-mouthed bottles and jars was developed. In 1903 Michael J. Owens of Toledo patented a fully automatic bottle-making machine. By 1912, a significant amount of Whitall, Tatum's production was machine-made.

The effect of the conversion to automatic production begins to appear in the company's post-World War I catalogs. By the early 1920's show jars and other elaborate wares are given much less prominence. By the end of the decade the variety of wares displayed has been drastically reduced. All the vitality seems to have been drained out of shapes and forms. The bottles shown are plain and strictly utilitarian. In the intervening years, Whitall, Tatum had mastered the production of milk bottles and electric insulators and battery tumblers.

The tendencies toward efficiency and uniformity, with the concomitant decline in any pretension to artistic quality, continued after the acquisition of the company by the Armstrong Cork Company in 1938. In 1940 the last of the company's hand production facilities were turned over to the Wheaton Glass Company, also of Millville. Wheaton continues the old traditions of glassmaking, and has developed a museum devoted to the study and exhibition of south Jersey glass.

Under Armstrong's management the facilities of the South Millville plant were expanded. Today, the plant, owned since 1969 by the Kerr Glass Manufacturing Corporation, is still one of the major producers in the country. The majority of their production is devoted to containers for beer and liquor, soft drinks, and baby and other foods.

Although the South Millville plant is still in production, the identity of Whitall, Tatum is only kept alive by the growing corps of collectors of nineteenth-century commercial glass. Even in the standard form of English Blakes or plain panels, these bottles, with their small irregularities in form and color, preserve the memory of an era when each piece of glass bore testimony to the individual blower's craft and skill.

Suggestions for further reading

general books on glass:

DAVIS, PEARCE. *The Development of the American Glass Industry.* Boston: Harvard University Press, 1949.
A thorough economic history supplying some data on the development of technology as well.

GROS-GALLINER, GABRIELLA. *Glass, A Guide for Collectors.* New York: Stein & Day, 1970.
A world history useful for placing American production in perspective.

KNITTLE, RHEA MANSFIELD. *Early American Glass.* New York: Appleton-Century, 1934.
Still a useful and very readable general history which contains much valuable information on early factories.

MCKEARIN, GEORGE S. and HELEN. *American Glass.* New York: Crown, 1948.

MCKEARIN, HELEN. *Two Hundred Years of American Blown Glass.* Revised edition. New York: Crown, 1966.

SCHWARTZ, MARVIN D. *Collector's Guide to Antique American Glass.* New York: Doubleday, 1969.

specific on bottles:

FREEMAN, DR. LARRY. *Grand Old American Bottles.* Watkins Glen, N.Y.: Century House, 1964.
Particularly strong on commercial bottles, with extensive reprints from catalogs of Whitall, Tatum's competitors.

KENDRICK, GRACE. *The Antique Bottle Collector.* Sparks, Nev.: Western Printing & Publishing, 1964.
A good capsule review of bottle types.

MCKEARIN, HELEN. *Bottles, Flasks and Dr. Dyott.* New York: Crown, 1970.
The story of the Dyottville (Penn.) Glass Factories. A most unusual chapter in American glass manufacturing history.

MUNSEY, CECIL. *The Illustrated Guide to Collecting Bottles.* New York: Hawthorn, 1970.
Information on the history, manufacturing, collecting and restoring of bottles.

VAN RENSSAELAER, STEPHEN. *Early American Bottles and Flasks.* Revised edition. Stratford, Conn.: J. Edmund Edwards, 1969.
A basic work, but with more stress on historical flasks than on later commercial bottles.

general on south Jersey glassmaking area:

BECK, HENRY CHARLTON. *Forgotten Towns of Southern New Jersey.* New Brunswick, N.J.: Rutgers University Press, 1962.

BECK, HENRY CHARLTON. *More Forgotten Towns of Southern New Jersey.* New Brunswick, N.J.: Rutgers University Press, 1963.
Both volumes, available in paperback, are popular histories of many villages and towns where glassmaking flourished in the nineteenth century.

current periodicals for bottle collectors:

The Antique Trader
Collector's Weekly
Hobbies
The Old Bottle Magazine
Spinning Wheel

Public collections of commercial glassware

The following public historical and art museums have indicated that they do have within their holdings more than a few pieces of late nineteenth-century commercial glassware—produced by Whitall, Tatum and other glassworks. Some of these items will be found on permanent display, others are included in period rooms, and, lamentably, yet others are in storage.

Whitall, Tatum collections:

New Jersey Historical Society, Newark, N.J.
New Jersey State Museum, Trenton, N.J.
Wheaton Museum of Glass, Millville, N.J.

other major collections of commercial glassware:

The Corning Museum of Glass, Corning, N.Y.
Toledo Museum of Art, Toledo, Ohio

museums with minor collections:

Brooklyn Museum, Brooklyn, N.Y.
Chicago Historical Society, Chicago, Ill.
Cincinnati Art Museum, Cincinnati, Ohio
Cleveland Museum of Art, Cleveland, Ohio
Fine Arts Gallery of San Diego, San Diego, Calif.
Florida State Museum, Gainesville, Fla.
Henry Ford Museum & Greenfield Village, Dearborn, Mich.
Metropolitan Museum, New York, N.Y.
Michigan Historical Commission Museum, Lansing, Mich.
Minnesota Historical Society Museum, St. Paul, Minn.
Missouri Historical Society, St. Louis, Mo.
Museum of Fine Arts, Boston, Mass.
Museum of History and Industry, Seattle, Wash.
New York Historical Society, New York, N.Y.
Ohio Historical Society, Columbus, Ohio
Smithsonian Institution, Fine Arts Museum, Washington, D.C.
Smithsonian Institution, Museum of History and Technology, Washington, D.C.
State Capitol Historical Museum, Olympia, Wash.
State Historical Society of Wisconsin, Madison, Wis.
Staten Island Historical Society, Richmond, S.I., N.Y.
William Penn Memorial Museum, Harrisburg, Penn.